BLUNDERBUCK

STARBIRD

PHOENIX

'regeneration'

Ethical Cleansing

GENIUS EDITION

Andy Gallagher

ASSAULT OF THE WHITE-TEMPLED PRECINCT

'In the mountains of truth, you never trump in vain'

COPYRIGHT 2021 Harvey Hufflewaffer Ink-Well

INTRODUCTION

Proceed at extreme **Caution**: contains very bad language

This book was produced on an independent publishing platform and is therefore "not a real book at all;" according to the stiffs at the nearby library desk anyway. Please be careful who you share it with as it cannot really be classed as 'proper' literature. The Author makes no apology for being such a freak-of-nature, and will not accept liability for any changes in personality, behaviour or levels of intelligence as a result of your reading experience.

Who's a pretty boy then...?

Dear Mr. Mayhew,

I'm going to call it a day with the Norfolk Constabulary. One of their cohorts did shuffle by a week or so ago to say they wouldn't be coming round again, so you may have had some effect. Let's hope they are telling the truth this time. I'd say they had no intention of answering any of my questions, but I do appreciate your efforts on my behalf. I'm happy to let them hoard their versions of the past, if it means they will stay off my back. Your friend Hal Turkman made a brief visit the other day (there was only one of him!), to check me out. I'd not been feeling well, but my eyesight was still up to recognizing him, hanging around the front door. If I'd known he was going to call, I would have smartened myself up a little.

Belinda's Hot Air   Violent rapist sentenced today!

By SARIN | Published: AUGUST 20, 2020 | Edit

"There's simply no explanation for what he's done..."

"I needed to hear all the sordid little details for my peace of mind."

'Hi hun, I hope you've had a productive time on-the-job. It can't be easy working for twelve hours in a Care-home where the residents are all dropping like flies. I just wanted to compliment you on your body. It's very sexy, and all I would wish for. However, I've not been very well these last few years. I'm finding it more and more difficult to get aroused. I was so poorly two years ago that I decided to kick it all into touch. You might be better with someone a bit younger. I apologise for lying about my age. I wish you and your family well. I don't love you, but I send you my love, if that makes any sense...thank you for all the great memories.' **R.I.P.**

ILL le GaL SubStanceS

Popular fears, and learnt stereo-types

HOME

Welcome to one of the most unusual and intriguing sites on the net.

The Literature section comprises a number of different *HIVES* each containing a selection of short stories, poems, and political satire.

There is also a section involving **Prophecy** and **Prediction**, **Spells** and **Invocations**.

You can also order your own personalised **ASBO**.

I have long considered writing to be a *form of art.* The Artwork section contains pages from the *infamous* 'THUNDERBUCK RAM.'

BELINDA'S HOT AIR gives participants of the site the opportunity to express their views on a very diverse range of subjects. By clicking on the heading you can add your own comments, but you need to be signed in to *Facebook.*

'A place to pour your scorn upon the world.'

FIRST CONTACT is a forum for new untested artforms and experimental writing.

In an age of increasing state control and monitoring your general comments and feedback are positively encouraged.

OUR FREEDOM OF SPEECH AND LIBERAL VALUES HAVE TO BE PERMANENTLY FOUGHT FOR OR ELSE THEY ARE LOST.

Live dangerously and to your heart be true.

Proxima Centauri Alpha
LO+4A

Border-line personality disorder

4

Dear Gorgeous daddy,

Why did you ignore my texts and my wonderful offers of assistance when you fell down the rabbit hole? H has been extremely upset at the way you just crashed on the floor, causing him to trip over you several times. You have caused us both so much pain and distress it is breaking my heart. The Queen has been very supportive and thinks you should get a nice warm bath now you are feeling a lot better.

We are fed up of Willy thinking he is King already. If we want to get a stupid little jerk into hot water for intruding into our privacy it is up to us. I am furious at the things they have written about me. Even the bishop makes up stories. He's as mad as a march hare, but then he is a member of the English clergy. Where is a knight in shining armour when you need one...? Do you still think I'm prettier than Alice?

I don't believe she likes me one little bit. We are both very different people underneath. I am a talented actress. She is as dull and boring as dish-water. I've been practising my smile for hours today.

H has bought me a new diamond broach and a tiara. We're having the spare cottage decorated, with a few new chairs for the lounge.

I think it's time we did some gardening. We could really do with a nice duck in the pond. The frogs are coming over to see us after lunch.

Love you with all my front covers, but please keep your distance!

DARLING MEGAN XX

GETTING HIS CHOPPER OUT

'If you give a monkey a gun, sooner or later, it's gonna shoot somebody...!'

Small brown monkeys

Caught red-handed,
On the case,
In a state of hurried confusion,
Climbing like acrobats,
Down the back of the frame.

Stolen from poor Gertrude,
Who watches motionless,
From the concrete floor below,
The three youngsters,
 gorged in the bag.

Through the rotten entrance,
for winter's feast,
The chinks of invading light,
Splash like comets.

Under the cooker,
A pair,
Of glittering brown plates,
Peer into mine.

The Foot-tapper

Tapping away,
The days of your life,
In the A-stream,
Unable to keep still.

Mr. Roache points to the blackboard,
And turns to stare,
Towards the door,
In amazement.

Where the Foot-tapper,
Increases his beat,
Drumming away,
With the heel of his shoe.
On the chair-leg.

A deadly silence,
Then Hibbert sniggers;
"You madman!"

Teach you a lesson you won't forget!

DaVE WaLLiaMS sayS....

By RUMPLESTILTSKIN | Published: JANUARY 27, 2020 | Edit

I'll make Piers Morgan eat his words, if it's the last thing I do before breakfast.

ACTOR HUGH GRANT aDMItS;

"I'm all washed up. It's completely over for me now. Leaving Europe was a catastrophe, but having a blow-job in the front of the car was fine."

CAR SHOW ROOM

By ADUMLA | Published: JANUARY 26, 2020 | Edit

Little Shitzah: "I've had the Norovirus. He hasn't given me anything to eat for three whole days now."

It's in the Just AYLSHaM aLReaDY? MY, JonatHan CERtainLY KnoWS HOW to PuLL StRings. No, I JUSt WOnDeReD IF YOU tHOUGHt it WaS a nICE PICtURE. It WaS tHE OnE taKEn BY HIM LaSt MOnDaY WHERE I aM LOOKInG aCROSS at tHE WaLL....HaHa! BEInG On OnLY WatER SHOULD BE GOOD FOR YOU. WE aRE WatCHInG YOU to MaKE SURE YOU DO nOt BREaK YOUR VOW! I'M nOt SURE aBOUt tOMORROW EVENInG YEt. I MaY JUSt SaY a QUICK HELLO. I'M nOt LIKE YOU In OnE RESPECt. I Can OnLY COPE WItH a LIMItED aMOUnt OF GaMES. I aCtUaLLY FInD tHEM QUItE StRESSFUL, anD MEntaLLY EXHaUStInG. I'M StILL tRYInG tO GEt a COPY OF MY MILLS GaME tO BRInG It aLOnG nEXt WEEK, aFtER LEaVInG It BEHInD On tHE taBLE In MY EXCItEMEnt.

Love from Andy xxx

PIGS ALWAYS LIKE TO LIE...

By BIRD DUNG | Published: OCTOBER 4, 2019 | Edit .... in crap.

Sergeant Matt: "Everybody liked him, even those he arrested..."

Hi Andy – I've reviewed my scoresheet and have transcribed it below – as I find so often, it doesn't make complete sense, but you may be able to correct my hand and turn it into an accurate record of the game. If you succeed, please let me know!

1. d4; d5
2. e4; Nf6
3. Nc3; e6
4. Bg5; Be7
5. e5; N(f6)d7
6. Bxe7; Qxe7
7. Qf3; O-O
8. O---O; c5
9. Nb5; Nb6
10. Bd3; c4
11. Bxh7; Kxh7
12. Rd1; a6
13. N(b5)c3; Bd7
14. h4; Na4
15. Kb1; Nxc3
16. Nxc3; f6
17. Qh5+; Kg8
18. Rh3; Be8
19. Qg4; f5
20. Qg5; Qxg5
21. Pxg5; g6
22. Rh1; Nd7
23. Rh8+; Kg7
24. R(h1)h7 checkmate

ROD:

This cannot be an accurate record of all moves, as (1) on White's move 12 the rook is already on d1 – so did you move it to e1 at that point? and (2) on White's move 16, the knight capture is impossible since I haven't recorded your second knight as having moved from its home square. I don't know at what point I failed to record your knight move (and my reply) – any ideas? Start playing draughts?

You played alright Rod. I hustled you when I put your king in check with my rook and said it was check-mate next move, just before you resigned.

FORTY-YEAR-OLD PHILIPINO WOMAN LOOKING FOR RELATIONSHIP

PigS LiKe vieWing porn

YOU NEED HELP

WE ONLY WANT TO HELP YOU

POLAR BEARS TOO WHITE

Convicted Sex-offender cripples the House of Windsor

By PETER SMITH *| Published: JANUARY 28, 2020 | Edit*

It has been reported to me today, here at HQ, that Prince Andrew is burying his head in the sand, and refusing to co-operate one iota.

1 He refuses to talk about how many times victims were shagged rotten by their perpetrators at the Epstein mansion.

2 He still insists that many of these girls were willing participants in an orgy of sex, debauchery and filth.

SHAME ON YOU PRINCE ANDREW!

READY WHEN YOU ARE JEFFREY

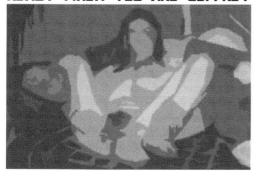

Death rattle of the Midgard snake

Under my skin,
The death sound,
Of the Midgard snake,
Fills my head with heavy rock.

Rattles its way inside my skull,
Destroying all the lucid thoughts I had.

I lie in the gutter,
Hearing the noise,
Of its hideous wheezing,
Clogging my lungs.

Is it my freedom?
Have I become,
Too long in the tooth…
To ever think about heaven…

'If success were judged by how many babies you could pop out then some of the most ignorant and selfish people on the planet would be considered its highest achievers…' KEEP HIDING YOUR FACE JOE!

Over 70 million U.S. Citizens incapable of making a rational decision….?

RACIST ABUSE BY BULGARS

ADUMLA | Published: OCTOBER 15, 2019 | Edit
That's disgraceful. Shouldn't be allowed!
George Herbert

Watson quits as deputy: thank fk

Kindle Team Support,

Thank you for your continued help and support. It is greatly appreciated. Three days ago I made some changes to a cover and also made a slight change to the description. My changes were saved and the book approved. The change to the description went through straight away. You asked me to wait three days and the changes to my cover would go through, but they haven't, so I have done it again. It saved my changes to the cover once again. I then approved the book for publication. I am very anxious that the changes go through alright and that the correct version appears On-site without further titles disappearing from my bookshelf.

THE BANNING OF FACE-MASKS
By SARIN | Published: OCTOBER 4, 2019 | Edit

Due to the unprecedented rioting on the streets of Hong Kong Carrie Lam has decided to ban the donning of head gear which: prevents the Authorities from recognising who you are, storing your image forever on their computer, and pursuing you for the rest of your life. Students familiar with the concept of 'freedom' are on the front-line. Of course, who am I to encourage people to break the law? Breaking the law is 'bad.' It could get you a bad name. It might even mean that you will never be able to get another job or end up in a bad place. It's okay for *pigs* to wear them though...

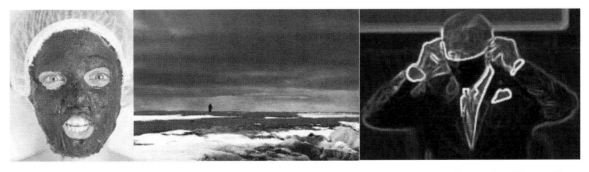

Trump says; "I feel a lot better!" BBC say…"No, he doesn't!" (fight the illness!)

The new domestic abuse bill

By GODFREY WINKLEBACKER | Published: OCTOBER 3, 2019 | Edit

Yet another way to stereo-type men as rapists, aggressors and abusers. Another one-sided version of the truth.

Politics at one on the BBC

By GODFREY WINKLEBACKER | Published: OCTOBER 3, 2019 | Edit

"We've always asked: what would it take for the public to turn against Trump"

Which story shall we run?

By BIRD DUNG | Published: OCTOBER 1, 2019 | Edit

- Mad Harry follows in the footsteps of dear old mum
- Katy Price gets a new cut and blow-dry
- Gay Vicar is also a member of the Secret Service
- Corbyn owns a Rottweiler which hates Jews
- People who voted for Brexit have sub-normal intelligence
- William Hague unable to father children
- Doctors and nurses are vastly under-valued
- Black people have far less chance of finding a job than white people
- Library and media censorship

iN-THE-BuTT

1 All the car documents have vanished and I need to get a new M.O.T.
Would you mind asking her what she's done with them? I can't get through.
2 When you do come over, just to repeat what I already said; it would be
nice if you could take over mum's care for a day or two, just to give me a break.

The Plebs

By BIRD DUNG | Published: SEPTEMBER 30, 2019 | Edit

The Plebs were sitting on the sofa, when they asked me if I was in a relationship, or intended to be in one. I said there was a married woman pursuing me for sex, but I wasn't going to tell them her name in case they went round there and kicked the crap out of her.
I showed them a photo of Kath.......
Look, if you give her seven or above out of ten, I promise to screw her!
Comments

Oscars 'too white'

By USULI TWELVES | Published: JANUARY 13, 2020 | Edit

"Shocking!" says child serial killer. All sections of society should be misrepresented.

Hattie Carroll

Not as thick as you think

By ADUMLA | Published: SEPTEMBER 26, 2019 | Edit

Labour MP's are vowing *never* to back Boris Johnson over Brexit, because of his bad language. Oh, fk off will you!

Turkish mortar attack kills child

By BIRD DUNG | Published: OCTOBER 10, 2019 | Edit

Trump wanted for murder…

Colonisation of the planets

By RUMPLESTILTSKIN | Published: SEPTEMBER 26, 2019 | Edit

Observing the fighting and shouting in the House of Commons today made me think how wonderful it will be when our species has finally made its way across the Galaxy to set up home…

Nancy Pelosi shrieked

By SARIN | Published: SEPTEMBER 26, 2019 | Edit

It looks as though President Trump has made a serious error, asking for information against one of his sworn enemies. He was allegedly offering a bribe. How do we know this? Because a Democrat ear-wigging on the phone overheard the conversation and decided they would like a new penthouse.

President Trump has shown great statesmanship around the world and considerable leadership where it mattered most.

This comes at a time of great confusion.

AMERICAN DIPLOMAT FLEES 'JUSTICE'

By USULI TWELVES | Published: OCTOBER 7, 2019 | Edit

"This is a *human* problem"
"Why can't she just apologise and receive a nice comfortable prison sentence that will ruin her life?"
"This is not what immunity was meant for"
"We are a broken family!"
"Harry was a 'fighter,' and we are trying to honour his name"
"We are just getting through from hour to hour"
"How can someone be allowed to just get on a plane?"
"We need to get to know her before we can grieve"
"All we need to do is 'see' her"
"We need answers"
"We are not a bad family. We are just 'normal'"
"We just need to see your face"

CARRIE LAM

By SARIN | *Published: OCTOBER 8, 2019* | *Edit*

Unless I am very much mistaken, Carrie Lam is a thoroughly decent, intelligent, normal lady. The last thing she must want is people injured and fighting on the streets. I really don't know what can be done to get out of this mess. The Chinese Government have one opinion, and the Hong Kong students have another. I feel very sorry for her.

WORLD CHAMPIONSHIPS

JUST ONE HUNDREDTH OF A SECOND BETWEEN THE RUNNERS, AND THE VICTOR CELEBRATES. SURELY THIS MUST BE DEEMED A DRAW?

 **Comments**

ISN'T MANKIND TERRIFIC...

By USULI TWELVES | *Published: SEPTEMBER 25, 2019* | *Edit*

I watched a farming programme tonight where the vet cut off the testicles of five exuberant little male piglets.

"It's for their own good," they said. "It needs to be done. They were starting to show signs of aggression."

The poor little creatures screamed and wriggled like hell.

Without mankind around they could at least have a chance of leading a normal natural life.

Perhaps one day, mankind itself will be neutered. We can only live in hope...

SHIT–IN–THE–BUTT

By RUMPLESTILTSKIN | *Published: SEPTEMBER 27, 2019* | *Edit*

I took mum along to the Docs and was eventually allowed in with her.

She admonished me for making the appointment and said that I was not her 'real' son. Dr Moweku asked her if she would like to do a memory test with him. She said I was after her bungalow. We tried several ways to get her to co-operate, but she said that she knew what we were up to. She did get the day right when he asked, but she still refused to say anything about where she was hiding all her shoes, my clock, the hospital appointment letter etc. Eventually we gave up. Mum started talking about a pain in her shoulder as a way of deflection. The Doctor fell for it immediately. Managed to get her wedged on the floor of the car. Her arse just wouldn't move.

The D.A.P.O.

By SARIN | Published: OCTOBER 2, 2019 | Edit

Get your man labelled for life.

JUDGE for yourself…

TRUMP SEEKING DIRT ON BIDEN
It's easy to find dirt on Biden. Just look behind his ears!
Edit or delete this

Prince William and Harry ok!

By PETER SMITH | Published: JANUARY 13, 2020 | Edit

It's Andrew we can't bear to be near.

Iran says…

By PETER SMITH | Published: JANUARY 13, 2020 | Edit

Trump guilty of air-plane killings for failing to live up to his obligations.
"It's a great deal for our proud nation though."

There's a funny smell in our kitchen…

By PETER SMITH | Published: SEPTEMBER 25, 2019 | Edit
Is Swapper in town?

NO VOTER FRAUD IN OUR COUNTY

'If you go to a Supreme Court, and ask them if they have the power to intervene, of course they are going to say YES! As every Politician knows; its all about POWER. We all know what this is for. Boris Johnson prorogued the house to prevent Parliamentarians who didn't want to leave from fudging, dragging their heels, and from constant repetitive delay. They've had three years to talk about this and nobody is getting anywhere. We already know where they stand. The strutting peacocks of Parliament will be preening and patting their wings for the spotlight now the poxy Establishment pricks have made a decision. Who on earth takes this crap seriously anyhow…It would be interesting to hear what Nigel 'the racist' Farage has to say, if he's still allowed to speak in the media…oh, yes, he's a 'racist' dear people, for wanting to defend his own country from invasion.' LEE JUN FAN

THOMAS CROOK

'I would rather have been dead than meet this moment'

I waved to Sue

By BIRD DUNG | Published: SEPTEMBER 24, 2019 | Edit

I waved to Sue today, when I went in the library. She was at the desk. She doesn't like to be called 'Sue' she said.

That funny little guy with the red face was at his computer chair. He doesn't speak to me anymore and puts his head down if I see him now. He looks like a Brian, or a Rupert to me.

I waved to Sue, pointing across the floor, and said: "That's him!"

Heading: Mrs Begum

By RUMPLESTILTSKIN | Published: OCTOBER 6, 2019 | Edit

Fully approves of all be-headings
Spent most of her time lying on her back
A breeding machine for the good of the army
A poor innocent 'victim' of child abuse
Another example of the failure of the British State

Senior nurse McCard

By RUMPLESTILTSKIN | Published: OCTOBER 13, 2019 | Edit

The Little Shitzah was furiously cleaning the utility room just now.
"I've just done that!" I said.
"Don't you dare tell me how to clean up."
"I worked with Senior Nurse Mcard for twenty years..."

Trust idiots like the British pigs to steal people's parcels

By GODFREY WINKLEBACKER | Published: OCTOBER 8, 2019 | Edit

With the excuse that it could be a 'terrorist threat,' the British pigs have been opening people's private mail and snooping inside. Mail addressed to go to your intended destination is forestalled and slavered over by an increasingly large herd of knob-heads. Is there nothing the Government will not do to bend over backwards in support them...?

I saw you in the supermarket tonight

By RUMPLESTILTSKIN | *Published: OCTOBER 8, 2019* | *Edit*

I saw Sherie in the supermarket tonight. Of course, that's not her real name. She was sent to my writing group to serve as a stool-pigeon. I told her I'd got a new phone and that she was welcome to drop by for coffee anytime. She was dressed in black, and was buying a birthday card for her daughter. I noticed a chain and some keys swinging from her hips.

"I've got a new job," she smiled. "I'm working in Norwich prison."

"I wouldn't like to work in a place like that," I said.

"You might end up there if *you* ever misbehave," she laughed.

When Sherie first came to my group all she wrote about were rapists, stalkers and sexual deviants.

She asked me to keep her work in a safe place so no-one else could find it…

Vindictive phone calls

By BIRD DUNG | *Published: OCTOBER 12, 2019* | *Edit*

I've been getting vindictive phone calls from the Plebs for a few weeks now. I know its them. I can smell the urine and decaying vegetable matter.

"We know where you are. When are you going to get rid of those annoying posts!" a voice cries. Home Office I think. London accent.

They sent a car to see if mine was in the drive. I was at the chess-group you slithering devious lump-heads!

'Sherie' was at the supermarket again today. She'd smartened herself up and was wearing make-up.

"That's two days running you have sloped past me in here. I'm beginning to think you're following me…"

She smiled. At least I got a hug this time. Nice face nice tight little…

THE RIGHT TO WEAR MAKE-UP IN THE ARMY

ZULU WARRIOR

'Try our new toothpaste, and brush like a pro'

Government furlough scheme approved by spin-doctors

I've just spoken to a Christian...

By GODFREY WINKLEBACKER | Published: OCTOBER 21, 2019 | Edit

Who believes he has died nine times, and that his physical body will be restored to health by Jesus, at the time of the second coming.

THE CREATION OF THE BRITISH NATION

THE CASTRATION OF PETER ABELARD

By PETER SMITH | Published: OCTOBER 21, 2019 | Edit

For those of you who 'don't know:' Peter Abelard was a Catholic priest and philosopher during the Middle Ages. He became a lodger in Canon Fulbert's house in order to teach his niece about the *facts of life*…and thus began a fateful and tragic love-affair. Heloise became pregnant, so Abelard sent her away in secret to be looked after by his own family. Fulbert arranged for a gang of henchmen to go round to Peter's house in the middle of the night and take away his two prized possessions. All the people involved in this story of hypocrisy and subterfuge were adamant Christians, who believed in absolution, forgiveness, and the sanctity of the soul.

Guilty as sin

Jo Swinson complains...

By SARIN | Published: OCTOBER 17, 2019 | Edit

"The PM is trying to *rush through* Brexit by holding the country to ransome"

RESPECT!

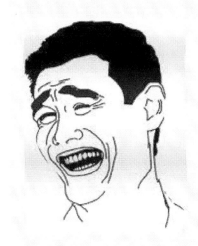

"Who gives a fuck about Christmas..."

Transgender games

By BIRD DUNG | Published: OCTOBER 18, 2019 | Edit

A new Olympic games are about to begin. For all those poor sods who can'd decide what they really want to be. We need to make everyone more 'normal.' Women should be allowed to walk on the Moon....

If Gaza did not commit any kind of assault...

By PETER SMITH | Published: OCTOBER 17, 2019 | Edit

then why did the police charge him with it?

19

"A very difficult mob!"

No sign of the idiots on the Courtroom steps claiming Gazza was the most dangerous man ever to put on an England vest? What a surprise. Conspicuous by their absence...you *bags of shite.*

The Swinson and Corbyn affair

By PETER SMITH | Published: OCTOBER 17, 2019 | Edit

'We will do everything we can to scupper this new deal. We would rather die in a ditch in the road, than let it go through'

Cardinal Newman revitalises church reputation

By SARIN | Published: OCTOBER 14, 2019 | Edit

"The Catholic Church holds it better for the Sun and Moon to drop from Heaven, for the earth to fail, and for all the many millions on it to die of starvation in extremist agony … than that one soul, I will not say, should be lost, but should commit one single venial sin, should tell one wilful untruth, or should steal one poor farthing without excuse"

- duped the broke and ignorant
- lived the life of a fat-cat on the Catholic pay-roll
- made a career out of spinning tales
- quit his job as an Oxford Don to pursue 'higher' goals
- gave everyone the creeps who met him

along with three candle-loving sisters
and a lay-woman, were:
MADE 'SAINTS' TODAY, BY POPE FRANCIS...the Good.

Trump the 'Magnificent'

By USULI TWELVES | Published: OCTOBER 16, 2019 | Edit

'The American people are my priority. I will do anything to protect them, and this includes leaving the Arabs to fight among themselves, which is what they have always done. This is not an American war and neither is it my fault that people are being killed in the Middle East.'

HAPPY BIRTHDAY BOSTIK

I tHRaSHED tHE PantS OFF YOU tONIGHt!

Halosar trap

'Never say never, in politics or love'

By USULI TWELVES | Published: OCTOBER 23, 2019 | Edit

The bombastic Spanish Government...lock anyone in prison who fights for independence, and denies them a democratic vote, because they want to ruthlessly hold on to their territory. People tend to believe that anyone who **loses** must have made a 'mistake.' This is simply untrue. Authorities never want to discuss their hold on power. First, they will not talk, and when they do, what they say is full of lies. Governments don't really give a damn about democracy. They are all members of an elitist club which sticks to the status quo. When you challenge any one of them you are accused of 'breaking the law.' *Comments*

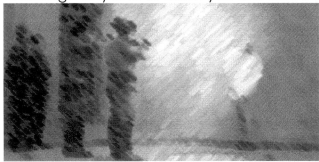

The powerful Un dynasty

By PETER SMITH | Published: OCTOBER 23, 2019 | Edit

When Kim Jong Un came to power he continued his Grandfather's ambition; to become a nuclear power, and therefore to have a seat at the richest most impressive table in the world. Jealousy fuelled his ambition. Greed fired the anger in his soul. His grandfather killed thousands of people but was spontaneously mourned by millions, as in the case of Uncle Joe. On seeing the affluence of the South he'd sent a squad of specially trained soldiers to cut off their leader's head, and bring it back to him in a carrier bag. Now, there's nothing wrong with murdering millions of people, just so long as you are the one calling the shots. This is the sort of thing you need to do if you are to be worshipped as a 'God.'

You look worried. Is something wrong?

leader of the pack

GRAND–MASTER GRINDROD

By GODFREY WINKLEBACKER | Published: NOVEMBER 8, 2019 | Edit

Beginning my game in the Swiss Rapid-play contest against the former International grand-master, after our formal handshake, I picked up the bishop and said…
"What do you call this piece again?"

AFRICA POLIO FREE

Dear Pain-in-the-butt,

I don't seem to be getting through to you. Mum doesn't want to go to church, especially not to be ignored by a set of two-faced lying gossiping chowderheads. She is about to start a course with Act to address her current needs. We don't need any food-parcels. Get back to Blarney will you.

Man sprayed pigs with petrol

By PETER SMITH | Published: NOVEMBER 8, 2019 | Edit
At least he didn't set anyone on fire.
But what a waste of Saudi piss!

"We wuz scared Your Honour."

I suppose wood will burn if you pour enough fuel on it.

Yep! Managed to do it again.

By ADUMLA | Published: NOVEMBER 10, 2019 | Edit

Knocked the coffee all over Tona's table.

STRUCK OFF.

ARMiStiCE DaY

By SARIN | Published: NOVEMBER 10, 2019 | Edit

We celebrate today, the time when our soldiers gave up their lives, so that we could enjoy and keep our 'freedom…'

Harvey Wine-stain, exposed himself to women

By USULI TWELVES | Published: NOVEMBER 10, 2019 | Edit

TOFF

Corbyn green tie date

By SARIN | Published: OCTOBER 30, 2019 | Edit

Thought that would get you!
Pain-in-the-butt again.
Giving us lectures on how we should keep the house clean.
"You don't even keep your own house clean…" I said.

The length of Gaza's tongue

By ADUMLA | Published: OCTOBER 15, 2019 | Edit

I've heard from people who knew Gaza long before he became famous, or even, infamous, that when he was at school he could lick between a girl's toes without ever bending over.
That kind of ability could come in very handy, on the right occasion.

ATROCITIES OF THE BRITISH ARMY IN IRELAND

By RUMPLESTILTSKIN | Published: OCTOBER 8, 2019 | Edit

Supported by Government...

To: **Ruta Kriksciuniene** Oct 6 at 10:36 PM

I hope you did alright if you did go to the contest today. Heather said you were down as a Challenger. I might not see you with my eyes, but I know you are still there...

Love from Andy

DIPLOMATIC IMMUNITY my ass...

By BIRD DUNG | Published: OCTOBER 22, 2019 | Edit

Diplomats have been using their status to get away with crime since time immemorial, as everyone in Government knows. What is this sudden surprise, as if its never happened before? I don't think sending a truck-load of pigs to the States will solve anything or make anything any better. It was obviously a terrible *accident.*

The importance of free-speech

By PETER SMITH | Published: OCTOBER 26, 2019 | Edit

Once again, the Authorities are trying to suppress free-speech, with the excuse of 'terrorism,' and 'radical ideas,' being top of their list of taboos.
If free-speech *only* included populist work, then that would not be free speech!
Their answer: "We shouldn't let our poor young people hear any dangerous new ideas..."
Wow, Idris! Have you seen this? More greedy grasping humans to join us in combat!

PAIN-IN-THE-BUTT

By BIRD DUNG | Published: OCTOBER 26, 2019 | Edit

Mum scraped all her meal into the toilet today, just prior to wishing you good day and asking about the dog. Still crazy, after all these years. Well well...

Football killed Jeff Astle ●

By BIRD DUNG | Published: OCTOBER 26, 2019 | Edit

THE RELATIVES OF THE FOOTBALLER KNOWN AS JEFF 'ON-MY-NUT' ASTLE HAVE SAID THAT NO-ONE SHOULD HAVE TO GO THROUGH WHAT THEY HAVE BEEN THROUGH, AND THAT IT WAS A SCANDAL THAT GOOD OLD JEFF HAD BEEN ALLOWED TO HEAD A FOOTBALL DURING HIS PLAYING CAREER.
"HE'LL NEVER BE ABLE TO SEE THAT HE HAD ANOTHER GRANDCHILD," SOBBED HIS WIDOW. JEFF WAS SUFFERING FROM A FORM OF OLD AGE WHEN HE DIED...

Harvey Winestain exposed

By P. Pull Bollocks | Published: OCTOBER 25, 2019 | Edit

After being discovered in a wine bar listening to a comedian the arch-fiend, Harvey Winestain, was confronted by several furious females, who had heard about him on the news.

"Aren't you going to do something?" One of them shouted.

"Will someone do something?" another screamed at the surrounding audience.

I don't know if she was pleading with him to get his cock out or not, but if I'd been him, I'd have told the noisy bitch to fk off...!

Twin brothers

By SARIN | Published: OCTOBER 28, 2019 | Edit

"Knowing she had escaped to the States was like a punch in the face..."

SISTERS, aRE DOING it FOR tHEMSELVES

By SARIN | Published: OCTOBER 28, 2019 | Edit

Pain-in-the-butt was in the bedroom tonight.

"Will you get out! I came to see mum not you."

"And you need to mow the lawn!"

"Thank you for pointing that out," I said.

"I wouldn't have noticed if you hadn't mentioned it."

She spread her new coats over the eiderdown.

"I'm sure Uncle Chris is the Old cow's son," she whispered.

"There's madness in the family, I think."

Little Shitzah

By ADUMLA | Published: OCTOBER 29, 2019 | Edit

"Let's pretend to get on while she's here. That will really confuse her."

Bangladesh to be moved to Great Britain

By RUMPLESTILTSKIN | Published: OCTOBER 30, 2019 | Edit

Due to the rise in sea-level several million wonderful human beings will need to be rescued and found homes in Europe.

Finally got rid of pain-in-the-butt down at the station

By BIRD DUNG | Published: OCTOBER 31, 2019 | Edit

'That's it, finished,' she said. 'You're on your own from now on.'

'I'm going to be among normal people when I go home.'

'But you're not normal,' I said.

(Only here to look in the clothes shops)...

VIRUS ENTERING THROUGH EYES AND ANUS

Elephant man finds new disguise helmet and writes a short goodbye.

Trump wanted for murder

By RUMPLESTILTSKIN | Published: OCTOBER 30, 2019 | Edit

Driving on the wrong side of the road
Extremely un-popular with certain sections of the media
Winning an election
Not believing in global warming
Fondled someone's tits a century ago
Patted a dead billionaire on the shoulder
Tried to cover up an erection
Couldn't decide whether to buy a moped or a Harley Davidson
Said Corbyn was a complete waste of space...
Condemned fake news on CNN
Plainly spoke the truth
Broke with convention more than was necessary
Would not wear a mask and live in cave
"LAWLESS MISCONDUCT!"

By PETER SMITH | Published: OCTOBER 28, 2019 | Edit

The Duchess of Sussex was complaining about the press telling lies, twisting the facts, and carrying on a campaign of wanton persecution against their victim. If you are poor the press can say whatever they like, and no-one, not your local MP, or even Dixon of Dock Green, will lift a little finger in your defence.

No shoes for contest

By BIRD DUNG | Published: NOVEMBER 2, 2019 | Edit

When South Africa won the rugby union world cup final in 1995 there was only one black player in the team. Bluddy disgusting!

LIVE ON YOU-TUBE TONIGHT

- ❖ Baldridge forgets wig but not sleeping curfew
- ❖ Born again Christian cult
- ❖ Bee-keeper signs register accompanied by choir of angels
- ❖ Police gang call by for further training on porn web-sites

And many many more…

PELL

PERMISSION TO SPEAK MISS

THE Pain-in-the-butt rang to see what was happening over here. She ordered me to be quiet so she could control the conversation.
Apparently the Little Shitzah had hid the co-codamol behind the plants.

'Why did she do that?'

BUTT

i hope you are well   things just chugging along as 'normal'
We've been watching the World Championships   Was reading something in our local mag...
Power of Attorney might be something We need to think about for the future.
it Would save a lot of complicated Wranglings if mum ever became
unable to manage her own affairs. it Will happen one day. it's bound to if she lives on. I am
almost having to do it already, by arranging Work Which needs doing etc.... she doth protest, but
sometimes her judgement is impaired.
i would suggest; if We ever did it, to have us both as joint Custodians, With equal powers, in
Which case, neither could do anything without the other's agreement.... I think that as her natural
born children We should do this for her. it is more likely to Work if We Work together.
i have to tell you that it is getting harder to look after her.
i do a lot of this already of course, as I already said.
i would not want to pressurise her in any way and I think it is something that Will probably
Wait but not more than a few months at most....she's flushed her food down the lavatory again.

There's nothing for it...

By BIRD DUNG | Published: NOVEMBER 2, 2019 | Edit

We are just going to have to pay people to stay in their own country and donate our hard-earned resources abroad, in order to bolster their economy.

I finally managed to find the file. Shitzah and Jeremy 'Says-he's-a-car-mechanic' have been lying to me the whole time. I saw a bill, but it was wrong...firstly;

1 there was no accident

2 he omitted a cash payment made to him for a substantial amount

I hope mum hasn't been daft enough to pay him nearly seven hundred pounds.

He tried this stunt once before.

How are you supposed to get to the bottom of things if you can never get

people to tell the fking truth!

I am not taking the car to Jeremy again, and have booked it in for a service elsewhere.

Mum is the person who said she wouldn't take the car to him ever again!

She was awful last night and started throwing cereal all over the floor when she couldn't have her co-codamol...she had hidden the packet of 100 I got from the Chemist a few days ago.

I ordered some more, which were delivered today. she was grinning at me when I came back from shopping. I rang the Chemist, and she had hidden them again...they told me they had to hand the box through the window because she would not open the front door to them.

The door was actually open when I came home.

She said she would report me to the police if I took her tablets again, or let people into the house without her permission.

A couple of days ago two doctors called, at her own request....

Apparently they gave her the all clear. She is free to do what she likes.

GRETA THUNBERG

Did you see her petulant little face when the Monster walked by! Can you imagine being in the same school. Her head would hardly fit through the door. *Comments*

Prince Andrew

By GODFREY WINKLEBACKER | Published: NOVEMBER 16, 2019 | Edit

Only went to see his friend Jeffrey Epstein to tell him they couldn't be friends anymore. It was a good flight, with clear visibility, and plenty of nice grub on board.

The murder of Dalian Atkinson

By USULI TWELVES | Published: NOVEMBER 7, 2019 | Edit

These farmyard animals certainly like testing out their torture toys. No identities please! It may infringe on our privacy, and anyway, we don't like having our photograph taken.

The Vicar's wife

By BIRD DUNG | Published: OCTOBER 31, 2019 | Edit

Went with the Vicar's wife to the Feathers in Wymondham. He's retired now, but still spinning out sermons.

"Asian people are only good at maths because they learn everything by repetition..."

"You mean, like a parrot?" I said...I said.

The kiss of life
By BIRD DUNG | Published: NOVEMBER 2, 2019 | Edit

When Gazza was arrested for giving a "fat lass" a kiss on the train and accused of sexual assault, people abroad must have been scratching their heads a little. In Italy men kiss each other on the mouth and no-one says a thing...kissing has always been an expression of friendship. Why didn't the woman concerned just put it down to the silly behaviour of a very juvenile, drunk, middle-aged has-been...instead of making his life even more miserable? Its not a nice thing to happen if you didn't ask for it, but sometimes you just have to forgive someone.

I've been saying this for years, but here it is again:

By BIRD DUNG | Published: NOVEMBER 2, 2019 | Edit

Hate is not a crime.

Neither is disliking someone.

The idea that we should never 'hate,' and that we should love everyone, is an idea spread around by Christianity, a religion which has stood truth on its head.

Punishing people for a *feeling* shows just what a dishonest and petty society we are living in.

If someone calls you a name, then simply tell them to 'shove-off,' or something even better.

'Hate' seems to be quite a primitive emotion. Its not usually 'hate,' which people are talking about at all.

There will always be disagreement and dispute. That's just life. We can't be forced to like someone, just because the law says we must.

Justice for Harry

By PETER SMITH | Published: NOVEMBER 12, 2019 | Edit

Trump murdered our son.

Uncle Chris By PETER SMITH | Published: NOVEMBER 12, 2019 | Edit

"Margaret would never behave like that."

Not enough light through the window

Pam said,

when she saw my new motor-home,

Parked in the drive-way,

That it would block out the light,

going into Adam's Study,

and that he would not be able to see his

computer properly,

even wearing his spectacles.

I heard they moved a tree from the path outside,

For the same reason,

And that an appeal to shift one of the street lamps,

Was being heard at this very moment.

While I stood at my window,

Looking into the sun,

My shades in a drawer at home,

And the bars, painting my skin

With shadows.

PAIN-IN-THE-BUTT

I have also found the plug to my razor and my trimmer missing.
It seems likely she went snooping round my room with Kevin while I was at my
chess group. If I don't get them back that will be a new razor and trimmer she
owes me. I can't use them without being able to charge them up.
If you ever find yourself telling lies or behaving in a bitchy way. now you know
where you go it from. I dreamt about you last night, which is very unsual.
You were coming up some stairs, when I threw a book at you, knocking you
completely unconscious. I had to pick you up and carry you upstairs.

Prince Andrew 2

By MARTIN IGGER | Published: NOVEMBER 16, 2019 | Edit

Only went to see his friend Jeffrey Epstein to tell him they couldn't be friends anymore. It was a good flight, with clear visibility, and plenty of friendly attendants on board.
The staff were wonderfully co-operative...
 "So, what did he actually do wrong?"
"He fucked a girl at seventeen."
"No, I mean, what did he actually do which was wrong?"

I'M A NAZI KILLER AND I'M PROUD

"Having sex with Nazi officers was fun, but killing them was even better."

No such thing as a 'sexual offence'

By Seamus PIG-SHIT | Published: NOVEMBER 17, 2019 | Edit

I spoke to Peabody down at the station today. He opened his cabinet and gleamed over his shoulder. "Best animal porn I've ever come across!"

'Whatever turns you on,' I said. 'Aren't you worried someone is going to find out? The two-faced hypocritical Establishment will not look kindly on your perverse preoccupation during copper time.'

'Me,' he laughed. '*Most of the porkers in here are a bit bent.*'

'But you didn't call me in to tell me that,' I said. 'That's old news!'

'Oh, fuck!' I said. 'You've not brought me in to ask for yet more dosh? Can't you do what you normally do and steal from the **pig's benevolent fund**...?'

My Marshall's badge glinted angrily in the strobe light.

'I've told you before. I will not donate any money towards a statue of Jeffrey Epstein.'

You do know, he's the most wicked person on the planet...

YOU WORRY ME...

THAT WAS VERY WORRYING.

'Let me milk you like a cow'

White can man

By SARIN | Published: NOVEMBER 5, 2019 | Edit

My friend Heather said a driver had cut in front of her going through town the other day. When she got home she rang the company number which was on the side of his van to complain he had 'used the wrong lane.' She told me that when you drove a company van you had to be very careful not to soil its reputation. I'm so glad we have decent upright citizens around like you! I couldn't help noticing how friendly she was with the retired pig at our club. She wouldn't tell me how long she had known him...

MARIUS ELAGABALUS 111

IF NIGEL FARAGE SAYS ITS NOT BREXIT, THEN IT PROBABLY ISN'T WHAT WE VOTED FOR. I WOULD RATHER BELIEVE HIM THAN ALMOST ANY OTHER PERSON. NEITHER DO I WANT TO BETRAY BORIS JOHNSON. PRESIDENT TRUMP SAID THE UNITED STATES COULD NOT MAKE A TRADE DEAL WITH THE UNITED KINGDOM BASED ON WHAT WAS AGREED IN THE DEAL... SO, WHAT DO WE DO?

Dear Heather,

I can see why you like your sweet little weather clock. Did I tell you about the rainbow-maker I bought in Oxford (of course) which you attached to your window, and which moved round by the warmth of the sun's rays, casting a myriad of colours in different locations. When I arrived at the club a lot of them were at a big table downstairs, playing a few games, against a few newbies. David Love and Jonathan said hello. So did Pete. Was a bit reluctant to use the fishing-pole on Mathew Perry in case he started crying. If only he'd followed the main line a bit more I would have really cooked his bacon.

Upstairs they had a game lined up for me against Callum. He just did not reply in the way he was supposed to!!! lol He tied me in knots so I couldn't get my pieces out, which was very clever of him. In one manoeuvre he captured my rook. I thought about resigning then, but carried on. I was getting absolutely mauled. Crucified. By the time he had my king cornered he had a Queen, two rooks and a bishop all aimed at him. I only had my Queen and a rook left by then, but I hoped to make it as hard for him as I possibly could. In the end I resigned, with just my Queen left, against his Queen and rook. An interesting game. My writing went funny again. I'm hoping to have a bluddy good one before bed, but it's getting harder all the time.

Wish I knew how he did it.

Hi Andy

Callum is a good player who has beaten players well above his grade in the past.
As for my own "relative" success, well I've learned a couple of simple openings that develop my pieces whilst keeping my King safe.
And I've been watching You-tube tutorials and games.
Thats it, could just be a "flash-in-the-pan" time will tell!
Cheers, Pete (Thanks for the old joke)

AREN'T PEOPLE LOVELY

What do Christmas lights have in common with Jeffrey Epstein?   They don't hang themselves...

Man sprayed pigs with petrol

By PETER SMITH | Published: NOVEMBER 8, 2019 | Edit
At least he didn't set anyone on fire.

Named after Pete 'Tubby'

A selection of Anglo-Saxon weaponry. Even the helmet could be used to great effect. Banned from the streets of London until further notice.

Man up! Will you.

HI Andy

Aaww, we didn't win any prize money, just a paper trophy and a box of Celebrations chocolates, which we donated to the next raffle. Bostik and I put in £10 each as it was all for TearFund charity – we were also expected ... err ... encouraged to bring food for the FoodBank there.

You and I would make good quizmates, then, as I know nothing about any of those – I'm more on the science, languages, natural world, etc.

I don't do Facebook but I do do lots of rubbing.

At present I don't have a game for tomorrow, but I'll probably go to Broadland rather than Aylsham as it's cheaper on the petrol, and on the drink (50p), unless anyone from Aylsham wants to play a scheduled game, or unless David Elsey is going and takes me. I'm lunching with Charles tomorrow so may not rush back and might not go out in the evening anyway. I do hope the dreaded cramp monster will let me sleep tonight. Sally and Dannie are going to Cambridge today, so far as I know, and he's having tests and assessments starting tomorrow. You're right, it's so unsettling and worrying for her. Tona has extensive experience of medical matters and seems to think it best if Dannie doesn't have the transplant, as he would be going through enormous trauma, which he may well not survive and, even if he does, the rest of his life will be far from comfortable or plain sailing after it. There's always the chance of rejection of the new liver at any time and the drugs he'd have to take to prevent that have many unpleasant side effects. Dannie has always been emotionally fragile, as well as physically, so it would probably be best if he gets turned down and can enjoy the rest of his life in a natural way. But yes, both Sally and Dannie are going to need all their mental strength, either way. Dannie's foot has swollen to twice its normal size and he's beginning to smell. Hmm, hope your dream doesn't come true ... there again, if you knock a cup over in a dream, you don't have to mop it up! The ulcers are a lot better today, thank you, though not completely gone. I would have liked a baby by you, if only my ovaries were still there.

Love from Heather x

Dear Tom (Mr Horton) January 2021,

The last thing I want is any more trouble. I hope we haven't stirred up a hornet's nest. I didn't ask for Chloe to pass my letter on to you, but, hey ho...!

I just want to get on with my life. Please apologise to Mr. Mayhew for any trouble I have caused. If he has read my letter I wonder what he thinks. The police are very good at obfuscating the waters and constantly bringing things up from the past, which were over and done with decades ago.

This sorry business has been going on for many years.I could tell you a lot more about what it has been like, and some of the lies that I've had to endure. I did originally go through the IPCC as Chloe Smith suggested about twelve years ago, but was invited along to the police station, only to be bullied and derided by one senior officer and two detectives sneering at me from above.I feel that you are very unlikely to get the truth, as these people stick together like glue. I fully understand how difficult it is for Mr. Mayhew to get involved, especially when the party are usually so strongly allied to the force. They have been snooping into my private correspondence for years by the way.

. Dear Cara/Kindle support,

I was told the changes would be seen on-line after 72 hours. I followed the instructions and saved, but was told my cover hadn't been saved, so was left wondering why. I was instructed to start again, and save my cover. It still didn't work after another 72 hours. As I originally said, my book, 'Curse of the Wallingford Stalker,' is appearing in a national magazine on Thursday, and I wanted the improved version available for people to buy. Now I have been told it could take up to ten more business days. Could you please ask a manager to look into this for me and find out what is going on...Is there any way you can tell me whether the changes have been saved correctly and whether it will definitely go through alright? Isn't there anyone there who can do this for me or who can help. Is there anyone down there who cares a jot anymore?

Dear Victor,

Thanks for your help and personal attention. A few days from now is too late. I was told my book details would up-date more than a week ago. Can you tell me why they haven't up-dated, when I followed all the guide-lines I was given? There seems to be a lot of different people involved in helping me get to the bottom of this. I said in the very beginning that I only altered a few details on the cover. This has nothing to do with the 'look inside' feature or thumbnails, or the internal file.

Surely there must be someone on the staff who could have put this right ages ago?

The evil Joe McCann

By ADUMLA | *Published: DECEMBER 10, 2019* | *Edit*

- ✓ Has received 33 life sentences 'for the good of the public.'
- ✓ Considered too dangerous ever to be freed.
- ✓ Refused to give evidence because he knew it would be an absolute waste of time.

Knew the police never told any porkies.

While McCann bought a packet of condoms one of his victims sat in his car watching the traffic.
As he booked a hotel room one of the people he is alleged to have kidnapped lounged in the passenger seat preening their hair.
While I believe what he did was wrong I would dare lay every penny I have that half the stories told about him are untrue.

PRIVATE DICK

.unt.

Interviewing people about their sexual preferences
Tracking down people and conducting reports
Going through legal or financial records for any dirt
- ✓ Verifying shit
- ✓ collecting evidence
- ✓ Following crime suspects or persons of interest
- ✓ recording their activities and whereabouts
- ✓ informing clients about body odour

Investigating computer related crimes, kidnappings, rapes, disappearances, homicides, suspicious activity, and theft by non-members of the Government.

Working in tandem with Law Enforcement offices:
- ➤ Sharing investigation results and findings
- ➤ interviewing detained suspects
- ➤ assisting in the investigation
- ➤ Updating clients on the progress of the investigation
- ➤ asking about further information for the investigation
- ➤ Investigate past activities and characteristics of a person
- ➤ Evaluate performance or honesty of employees of a company by posing as one or as a client

APPREHENDING CRIMINAL SUSPECTS OR CRIMINALS AND TAKE THEM TO THE AUTHORITIES
PRESENTING INVESTIGATION RESULTS AS EVIDENCE AND GIVING TESTIMONY IN A COURT-OF-LAW WHEN NECESSARY
TRANSCRIBING INTERVIEWS CONDUCTED
ORGANIZING EVIDENCE TO BE PRESENTED TO HIS HIGH AND FUCKING MIGHTY THE HONOURABLE ASS-HOLE

Interviewing people to gather information on a case.
Researching information relating to a case.
Doing surveillance work.
Going undercover to find information.
Collecting evidence to be used in a court of law.
Investigating crimes.
Handling legal documents and court citations.
Performing background checks on people.
Helping to find a scape-goat and put them behind bars.

Hi Heather!

Things seem a bit better today after the nightmare of last night. Best to stay calm. Not to take anything too seriously if you can. See it for what it is. I only spoke to Dannie for a short time but got to know him quite well. I didn't know it was him and Tona who started the chess group. I am playing in a match at the club, all being well. How are the magic mushrooms...?

Love isn't really love if it is one-sided. It needs to be reciprocated. Dannie is lucky to have so much support, but it will not prevent the inevitable.

It's so funny listening to you. We are so alike. I can even empathise with your money worries, having been in just the same position in the past. I find it hard to hold a grudge too.

If people don't really care about you you are better off without them!

We've had the same problem with our broad-band. If you get onto your provider they can usually boost up your signal!! Don't forget to look after the gold-fish.

I just thought you looked a wee bit tired. I'm sensitive. I notice things like that.

Was up early to go and get milk. Catching up with jobs and so on.

I hope you are having a good day, and keep up with the messages!!!

I hope you have your broad-band back in working order now. It was a nice morning together.

Can I ask you; are you worried about anything? Are you alright?

When I got back I found my mum had been in my room and taken things again.

We had a bit of a row, until I eventually found where she had hidden them.

Now she's threatening to call the cops on me for being abusive.

My mum's always done this sort of thing, even when I was a teenager.

38

Dear Andy

Thank you for your missive and kind wisdom. Yes, we are alike in many ways. You are right, I was pretty tired yesterday, and am so today. But I'm enjoying having a quiet day, just wash-tubbed a load of coats, blankets etc and put some on the line and some on racks. Keeping an eye on the weather! Rain is forecast at 3pm ...There are several other jobs I ought to be doing:
scanning,
guitar and bass practice,
phone Auntie (probably shall);
aquaria water-changing,
hoovering,
going over the fence to cut trees down,
weeding,
scrub loos (probably shan't!)

Loud shrieking and yowling from the garden a little while ago – Oliver the tabby-and-white cat from No.70 and the new black-and-white cat having a heck of a fight! (We say "a dust-up" where I come from.) I went out to break it up but they took no notice of me whatsoever. Oliver is a big strong cat and drove the other one off. He's a bit of a hooligan; a couple of weeks ago he was drinking rainwater from one of the tubs in my yard (always good for a laugh as he has to straddle it with all four paws and sometimes falls in), then turned round and emptied his stomach of the most enormous amount of sick in two great long heaps. Eeww, the most disgusting fishy cat-sicky odour. I cleared up what I could and swilled it over, but I could still smell it for days :p

a copy of the letter I sent to the Co-ordinator about the new dementia therapy group starting todayI think The Blobs do care about me, but they care about each other more. I suppose that is a good thing, seeing as they are now married! Yes, their love is reciprocated, as is mine.

Ah, the broadband is an actual fault on the line, apparently somewhere out in the street. The phone is affected, too, some of the time, though it hasn't gone right off, as the broadband does. Fortunately it's on at the moment and I hope it will stay that way until at least I have sent you this missive and also be on just after midnight, when I hope to get on ChessTempo and keep my Flame going – there are 282 days on it today, but miss one day's puzzle and it reverts to zero instantly. I hope the engineer will be the same one as last time ("Richard"), he was good, and a nice guy. BT have given me £45 compensation, gratefully received

Here's a game I played (as White against a Sicilian Defence) last year, not a graded one, but I think it might amuse you and maybe give you some ammo to use online: 1. e4 c5 2. Nf3 d6 3. d4 b6 4. Nc3 Nc6 5. Bc4 Bg4 6. Ne5 Bxd1 7. Bxf7# Apologies to Légall! (You know his Famous Mate?)

Just brought in the clobber from the garden – nothing has dried much ...

Sorry to hear about your bad night. I had a better night and am reasonably bendy today. All good wishes for the Match tomorrow night!

Love from Heather x

All well Heather, apart from being stung by a wasp in the garden just now. they keep meddling in my e mails. following me round town again yesterday. I had a good day with Mila on Monday. We went to Wells, and then spent some wonderful intimate time at home together. I am still not very well though and I'm thinking of finishing with her. as I said to my friend Roger, maybe I'm destined to have a load of fleeting relationships. some people are.

Trump has black roots himself. He hasn't dyed his hair for a few weeks now.

The launch of my career

By BIRD DUNG | Published: NOVEMBER 18, 2019 | Edit

Virginia Giuffre has really started life with a bang. I predict a long and varied career, with cheque-books being waved in her direction from now til doomsday. The thought of Prince Andrew shagging hell out of her at seventeen fills me with absolute loathing.

Epstein's victims to receive huge bonus-payment

By PETER SMITH | Published: NOVEMBER 20, 2019 | Edit

I see that Prince Andrew has been forced to resign from his royal duties. I thought it was by performing his royal duties that he was in so much trouble. However, there's still a possibility of throwing a little more mud in Trump's direction, especially if Hilary gets invited to the palace again.
It's essential that the poor 'victims' receive 'justice:' in the form of a huge hand-out, which will mean they are no longer poor of course.
If the Epstein estate is divided up that could mean over one million dollars a bonk. How about that for repentance…?

Missing and never found…

Hi Ruta,

I hope you are having a good week. It's cold out there now, isn't it! I won in my match against Rod Mills last night. It was a good laugh. Heather was there and a few others. Erikas looked a bit tearful the other night. Rokas got a bit carried away and started practising his karate kicks on me. Oh well. It will toughen me up! I will send you some more exercises when I have a spare moment…
😶😮😃🧍
Yep! I definitely softened old Rod up for you. I saw his dejected expression. He was utterly demoralised by the time he played you.
How did the Board-meeting go. Any other news?
I'm not trying to hide anything.   You can ask me anything!

Letter from the Prince

By GODFREY WINKLEBACKER | Published: NOVEMBER 21, 2019 | Edit

DEAREST GUDRUN,

We have shared many secrets in the past, including the number of times Fergie went down on me in the Royal Range Rover.

All we wanted to do was have a little fun. I wasn't cut out for married life. Simple uncomplicated sex was what we were after. With Jeff you could really be yourself. He didn't mind what you did as long as it didn't scare the goldfish.

None of the girls who attended the parties were ever forced to do anything they didn't want to. They were willing participants, eager to learn, eager to become my Royal Performing Mistress. Ginnie was my first. She loved rubbing shoulders with the rich and famous. For a time I loved her and didn't think about anyone else. The sight of her moaning beneath my superb and masterly thrusts greased my old caber into a rod of frigging iron.

Jeff wasn't perfect. Is anyone? He was like a bluddy machine. He could shoot all night without having a rest. A lot of people didn't like him. He had a great sense of humour and was very generous. I think it's an absolute tragedy that he died the way he did, in prison. In my opinion he didn't do anything wrong, but am I allowed to say so. He was hounded by certain individuals who disapproved of his open-ness and liberal life-style. These do-gooding hypocrites make me want to vomit. I couldn't go anywhere without the snoops following me. It's the same for anyone well known these days. They stand with their paw round their telephoto lens in the bushes a mile away. I've spoken to mummy, and she is very cross about what has happened. Charles is refusing to speak to me until I turn over a new leaf.

I wish the Establishment would all fuck off and leave me alone. I suppose that while they are sweating around my hairy bollocks they are leaving some lucky fucker all alone.

Men jailed for hoarding Viking horde

By SARIN | Published: NOVEMBER 22, 2019 | Edit

'Treasure-hunters, who found a Viking horde, and didn't declare it, have been jailed for upwards of eight years...' gloated a member of the fuzz outside the Court-room today.

"They failed to declare the loot within the stipulated fourteen days. A crime that makes me seethe with anger," he said, wiping the saliva away from his mouth.

"I expect they wanted to get rich, and to share the stolen coins among themselves."

"I didn't like the look of them anyway, and neither did the snooty ass-hole presiding over this fiasco."

"The horde was hidden by an army of Norse-men, at 3.55 in the afternoon, on 22nd August 865. We know this is correct due to DNA analysis and soil samples which were sent away to be examined."

"They tried to deprive the children of this great nation from the chance of getting a clearer understanding of history and of their forbears!"

"This is the most horrendous crime of its type that I have ever seen. These deplorable rats have got exactly what they deserved."

METAL DETECTORISTS LOOK OUT! WE ARE ON YOUR TRAIL!

CLIMATE JUSTICE

Children of Isis fighters to be rewarded with anything they want

By Ginger Vitus | Published: NOVEMBER 23, 2019 | Edit

And the opportunity to join Isis when they reach adulthood.
Another great decision by the creeping scum of the Establishment.
"Where the Government can help, it will do."
"they immediately recognised their family home when they arrived back..."

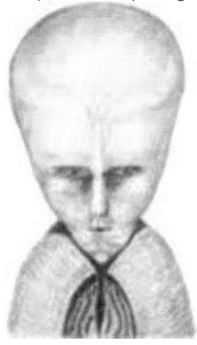

We Never did anything Wong!

I do believe in helping people and I often do, but in helping others, I also help myself.

Hi Virginija,

Thank you for a lovely evening in which we did some really worthwhile work.
I will get onto the rest tomorrow when I feel a bit better. It was nice watching on your phone.
I thought you looked very nice tonight. I am very lucky to be able to write, even though I don't feel as well as I used to. I do have a fair bit of free time, but now I find a lot of it is taken up looking after my mum. That's becoming like a job in itself! Friday next week is the Aylsham lights, and it will be brilliant. Ruta thinks you deserve a night off for a change. I think it would be great if you were all there. I am always here if you ever need a friend. I can't believe Bob tricked me like that...

Christmas humbug

By SARIN | Published: DECEMBER 18, 2019 | Edit

Decorations. What's the point. You only have to take them down again.

Conservatives guilty of on-line deception

By SARIN | Published: NOVEMBER 20, 2019 | *Edit*

The Social watch-dog 'Pussy-foot,' has uncovered new evidence today that the Conservatives deliberately tried to promulgate lies and untruths during last night's debate between the main parties.

This makes me so mad I could almost resign on the spot.

The BBC are rightly investigating why gay rights are not more of an issue in Lebanon…

I noticed three girls heckling Nigel Farage while he tried to tell them the truth.

I think you old saying is; you can lead a camel to water, but you can't make it drink…

 YOU'RE TOO KIND!

Hi Hayley,

I GOT HER UP IN GOOD TIME AND MEANT TO BRING HER IN, BUT SHE ADAMANTLY REFUSED TO GET DRESSED NO MATTER WHAT I DID. MY MUM'S ALWAYS PLAYED TRICKS LIKE THIS. IF SHE THINKS YOU WANT TO DO ONE THING SHE WILL DO ANOTHER. IF I'D TRIED TO COAX HER ANY MORE, SHE WOULD HAVE ENDED UP SHOUTING AND SCREAMING AND THROWING THINGS. IT'S NOT AS IF YOU CAN HAVE A NORMAL RATIONAL CONVERSATION TO EXPLAIN WHAT IS GOING ON. I NEVER COULD DO. HOPEFULLY, TOMORROW WILL BE DIFFERENT.

YOURS SINCERELY

Pain-in-the-butt: *now you know where you get it from.*

Eric from the library

By PETER SMITH | Published: DECEMBER 19, 2019 | *Edit*

Saw Eric from the library again, hurrying through town. I don't know what those two get up to. The runt was scampering a few yards behind him as usual.

Comments

Fake news….

By RUMPLESTILTSKIN | Published: JANUARY 8, 2020 | *Edit*

Sky News sides with Trump!

Censoring the dead

In the spring of the following year,
Like a model of devotion,
We filled your hands,
With new barbed wire.

In the name of freedom,
Discharged the floods,
And swept the earth,
Clear of perdition.

When men lie in the soil,
Like sleeping doves,
Never to see life again,
Or the faces of their beloved.

Squadrons of the fearless,
Linked to the ground,
by high commands,
Prayed for by devoted friends,
Hold fire,
And wait for your ascent.

And if it comes to the worse,
You can always pray to Jesus,
Break through the lines,
But leave no victims on the page.

In our lavish uniforms we cry,
The old guard out,
And the new ways in…
Clambering over runners on the sand.

In the places of the fallen.

Giving a speech at your daughter's fine wedding

I cannot imagine anything more ridiculous,
Than, giving a speech at your own daughter's wedding,
The sweet little anecdotes; when she first tried on some
Make-up, tottering along in her mother's high-heels,
Her long list of failed relationships, her tantrums…

We can smile now,
Here in this banqueting hall,
And you all laugh merrily,
Hearing my words:
how she came in my bedroom,
And scoffed my banana.

The wonderful Christian church

By RUMPLESTILTSKIN | Published: NOVEMBER 28, 2019 | Edit

In 913, after battling against the pagan Danes, the Mercian Queen, Aethelflaed, sensing victory, had her enemy cornered in a wood. Some of the fleeing Norsemen had gone in there to hide, fearing the wrath of their Christian foe. As they sheltered among the trees they heard the sound of axes chopping down everything around them. The merciful Queen, sensing her power and wealth increasing, ordered that her enemy be hacked to pieces and their lands confiscated for the church.

Saint David Duckenfield

By RUMPLESTILTSKIN | Published: NOVEMBER 28, 2019 | Edit

After thirty years of lucrative work for the legal establishment, at last we reach a fair and honest conclusion: NOT GUILTY!
A tragic accident which was not in any way due to negligence or mismanagement by the people in charge.
"Steady on lads. Only use your truncheons if absolutely necessary…"
"steel toe caps nicely polished?"
"We will provide you with a million of pounds worth of bullshit sir"
"they are only a miserable bunch of yobbos…"

HERD IMMUNITY

Epitaph: '*A wonderfully kind person. Always helping others. Completely unselfish in every single way…*'

Bollocks to Babylon bakers

Tory candidate caught on camera staging 'friendly' meeting with voter

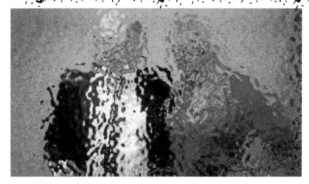

'THE RULE OF SIX'

Trump the 'Great'

By RUMPLESTILTSKIN | Published: NOVEMBER 28, 2019 | Edit

Supports Hong Kong citizens in their fight against oppression. Stick that in your pipes, you sycophantic drones of the Church of England establishment.

LONDON TERROR ATTACKER WORE SUICIDE VEST TO COVER HIS COWARDICE
We do not operate a shoot-to-kill policy in Northern Ireland

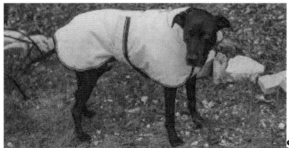

Sadly missed.

Baby chipmunk v Flash-Harry McClean
Sunday 17th November 2019

1. D4 D5 2. E4 DXE4 3. NC3 NF6 4. F3 EXF3 5. QXF3 NC6 6. BB5 A6 7. BC4 B5 8. BXF7+ KXF7 9. QXC6 BG4 10. NF3 H6 11. O-O E6 12. NE5+ KG8 13. NXG4 NXG4 14. QXE6+ KH7 15. QXG4 G5 16. QE4+ KG8 17. QE6+ KH7 18. RF7+ KG8 19. RD7#

London fights back!

By SARIN | Published: DECEMBER 1, 2019 | Edit

In the face of great evil ordinary citizens, with no links to the authorities whatsoever, are fighting back against the terror stalking the streets of the capital.

Tory budget cuts are thought to be responsible and not the warped cognitive distortions of reprobates, outnumbered by the ensuing mob.

"A cowardly act. He refused to have his nose rubbed in it."

"These people know how to do the right thing."

"London is good at that!"

"Try taking this fully loaded machine gun up the..."

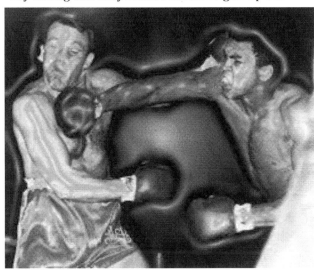

Nice jab!

STANDING UP FOR YOURSELF, A CAPITAL OFFENCE

Boris Johnson

By RUMPLESTILTSKIN | Published: DECEMBER 13, 2019 | Edit

Threatened with jail. Accused of being a groper of women who had a problem with women, a liar and a cheat. Blamed for all the problems in the Health Service. Reproached for trying to sell off the National Health Service. Branded a buffoon and an idiot. Denunciated for being a friend to the Donald. They tried every trick in the book to get rid of him but the people still voted for him in their millions.

By phone

By <u>BIRD DUNG</u> | *Published: DECEMBER 1, 2019* | *<u>Edit</u>*

Pain-in-the-butt: "I never read your e-mails."

Well, fuck off then!

Pain-in-butt

By <u>GODFREY WINKLEBACKER</u> | *Published: DECEMBER 4, 2019* | *<u>Edit</u>*

Mum says Michael fled abroad to get away from you, and I believe her.

A FAKE CHRISTMAS CARD

By <u>SARIN</u> | *Published: DECEMBER 4, 2019* | *<u>Edit</u>*

The Little Shitzah gave me an envelope addressed to me *and* her from the c..nts in Canada. She said it was addressed to us both, but when I looked closer she had *added* my name in a different coloured biro.

PAUL GAUGUIN. Sex offender!

Dear Internet Dogging Gang, I wish to report some very suspicious activity on my Time-line...

Doctors and nurses 2

By PETER SMITH | Published: MARCH 22, 2020 | Edit

'We feel 'compelled' to return to work in return for a nice fat pay cheque, and plenty of prestige...'

The sacrifices we have to make, for the good of society...

Trump visit

By ADUMLA | Published: DECEMBER 3, 2019 | Edit

"An affront to normal standards of human decency!"

Says pompous Oxford McVicar. **COMMENTS**

BOY FOUND SLEEPING ON FLOOR OF HOSPITAL

Johnson not fit to be Prime-Minister

By ADUMLA | Published: DECEMBER 10, 2019 | Edit

Shoved a newspaper in his pocket!

 I don't see the point anymore.

Ok campers! Who shall we wind up today?

Johnson only saw my son's death as an opportunity to make a political point

By SARIN *| Published: DECEMBER 11, 2019 |* *Edit*

RITTENHOUSE FOR MAYOR!

No she-wolf: Britain's favourite Queen

By PETER SMITH *| Published: DECEMBER 11, 2019 |* *Edit*

Having been married at the age of twelve to Edward the Second, to whom she bore many children, Isabella of France, then helped to see off the charming Piers Gaveston, who was rewarded for his years of service to the king by having his head removed from his body.   Seizing power with an Army of frogs and escorted by her new lover, she finally caught up with the wicked king, who she deposed, commanding her men to insert a red hot poker up his rear end, and then proceeded to punish his chief adviser, Hugh Dispenser, who was hung, disembowelled and castrated, while he was still alive, in front of the cheering and exuberant mob.

A Christian Queen you can really be proud of!

PERSONALITY OF THE YEAR (TIME)

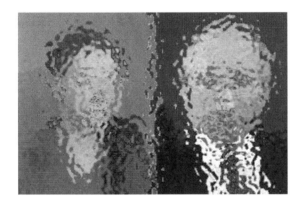

Corona-virus set to bankrupt Western economies

Hi Andy

We just were talking about you. I don't know if you have any plans for 24th December. Would you like to be a Santa Claus for our kids. We thought it would be a great fun. if you have any plans so no worries but if you free and would like to have fun in the evening with my crazy family from Lithuania you are welcome. We would sort everything, your outfit and the sack. you just need to turn up in the evening about p.m.

So, what do you think?

See, I always think about you as well.

Ruta

I know. It's the white beard...!

WRONG IS THE NEW RIGHT

Trump says Canadian President "two-faced"

By USULI TWELVES | Published: DECEMBER 4, 2019 | Edit

Human after all then.

Options for suicide

Jump from a bridge
Walk in front of traffic
Forget to put on your parachute
Go for a kip on a railway track
Detonate some high explosive
Criticize the Russian President
Fall from the end of a pier
Drink a whole bottle of bleach
Shoot yourself in the head
Stab yourself through the heart
Slit your own throat
Climb into a lion's den
Slice the end off your arm
Place your neck under a guillotine
Inject yourself with morphine
Jump onto a wooden stake
Hit a black mamba with your hand
Get married to the wrong partner
Hold up a bank without a face-mask

Head of Antifa threatens to pray for the President

By BIRD DUNG | Published: OCTOBER 2, 2020 | Edit

"My wife Jill and I regretfully send our condolences and hope you will keep your big mouth shut in future!"

"Look Doc. I've found a huge lump under my nuts. What the fuck are you going to do about it?"

£ Your application to renew your membership of the Social club has been denied owing to your *label.*

24ᵗʰ December 2019

Dear Prince Charles (and Camilla),

I hope you don't mind me writing to express my opinion on a very important matter.

I think it's terrible what has happened to Prince Andrew. How can a Prince Charming suddenly become a monster?

I remember during the Falklands war how the whole country was worried about him.

In my opinion Andrew hasn't done anything wrong, although his friendships were somewhat questionable. No human being on the planet is completely perfect. Andrew has, unfortunately, exposed his flaws to the world. He probably just wanted to have a bit of fun, and who can blame him for that. There is a lot of hypocrisy in this world, much of it in the media. It is often the people with the dirtiest hands pointing the fingers.

There are many people in prison who shouldn't be there. I do not believe in this trafficking story. These tales are often exaggerated anyway. Much of it is politically motivated. If I had been Andrew, I would have been completely honest, even if it was very uncomfortable for a time. People are not stupid. It will be far worse, in the long run, if the public think he is trying to cover something up. Having said that, I quite understand his reluctance to let a scheming young woman and the people around her use this opportunity to embarrass a Member of the Royal family. I don't know why she is behaving so spitefully unless she is being encouraged to do it by someone else. From what I have seen she did everything willingly and knew exactly what she was doing. The young women who Epstein invited along seemed happy to mix with the rich and famous. What kind of person wants to ruin someone's life?

As you probably appreciate, the most damaging disclosure was the photo of Andrew stood inside the door with what appeared to be a young lady leaving the house. It would not surprise me if someone like Mohammed al Fayed was responsible for getting the picture. He has harboured a grudge against the Royal family and Prince Philip for years.

I sincerely hope the Royal family can recover from this and that Andrew will find some love and happiness in his life to restore his good name.

May I wish you all a very Merry Christmas!

Yours Sincerely,

BUNDERCHOOK

- **PIS** Europeans inherited 2-4% of their DNA from Neanderthals, which gives them a greater immunity to colds and flu. Poor backward deprived Africans do not have any Neanderthal DNA at all which explains why more of them are succumbing to the virus. I am almost identical to a cave-man, except for the brow-ridges.

Miss World contest.

'Morally repugnant;' say bolshy clones performing in our classrooms.

She's got form!

Characteristics of "Witch" Trials

1. Pressure of Social Forces
2. Stigmatization of the Accused
3. Climate of Fear
4. Resemblance to a Fair Trial
5. Use of Simulated Evidence
6. Simulated Expert Testimony
7. Non-falsifiable Evidence
8. Reversal of Polarity
9. Non-Openness
10. Use of Loaded Questions

Traits of a witch...

Singing or breaking wind

Reading, but not from a bible

Refusing to conform

Not getting along with your neighbour

Living a solitary life

Writing

Wearing a long-pointed hat

Owning a broomstick

Having straggly hair or a beard

Having a wart on your face

Having a very hairy crotch

Owning a cat

Dancing naked in a forest or on the street

Unable to cry or feel pain

SUPERTAN

A nice compliment

By GODFREY WINKLEBACKER | Published: DECEMBER 7, 2019 | Edit

Paid a visit to the nearby supermarket this morning because the Little Shitzah had drunk all the milk during the night.

There's a beautiful dark haired lady called 'Cindy,' who's worked there for years, but recently she has put on a lot of weight.

As I rubbed my eyes at the check-out she was jigging around at the side of me in her Santa-hat. I just wanted to boost her confidence.

"Hardly recognised you!" I said. "Have you lost a lot of weight?"

"Are you trying to take the piss?" she replied.

Her work colleague rolled about in stitches.

Blessed be the Epstein

PRIMATE

Suffer the little children to come unto me.

ISLAND DWARFISM

Aren't people wonderful! Let's pray for them and get them all up to heaven...

Hi Heather,

Just sending this game I had 15/12/2019 against **Amar Khawaja** of Canada

I thought about resigning many times due to the hopelessness of my position. They were also a very tricky player. I've noticed that on Chess.com a lot of the players abort if they are playing black. I was playing black in this game.

1. **e4 c5** 2. **Qf3 d6** 3. **b3 Nc6** 4. **Bb2 Nf6** 5. **Bc4 Bg4** 6. **Qg3 h5** 7. **h3** Be6 8. **Bxe6 fxe6** 9. **Ne2 Nxe4** 10. **Qf3** Ng5 11. **Qg3 Ne4** 12. **Qe3 d5** 13. **d3** Qa5+ 14. **Bc3 Nxc3** 15. **Nbxc3 d4** 16. **Qxe6 dxc3** 17. **O-O** Nd4 18. **Nxd4 cxd4** 19. **Qc4 e5** 20. **Qe6+ Be7** 21. **Qg6+** Kf8 22. **f4 Qb6** 23. **fxe5+ Kg8** 24. **Qf5 Rf8** 25. **Qd7 Rxf1+** 26. **Rxf1 Qd8** 27. **Qe6+ Kh7** 28. **Rf7** Re8 29. **Qf5+ Kg8** 30. **Qg6 Bf6** 31. **exf6 Qxf6** 32. **Rxf6 Re1+** 33. **Kh2 Re2** 34. **Qxg7+ Kxg7** 35. **Rf4 Rxc2** 36. **Rxd4 Rxa2** 37. **Rc4 c2** 38. **d4** b5 39. **Rc3 a5** 40. **d5 b4** 41. **Rc4 Kf7** 42. **Kg3 Ke7** 43. **Kf4** Kd6 44. **Ke4 Ra3** 45. **Rxc2 Rxb3** 46. **Rc6+ Kd7** 47. **Ra6 Ra3** 48. **Rb6 Kc7** 49. **Rb5 b3** 50. **Kd4 Ra4+** 51. **Kc3 Ra3** 52. **Rxb3 Rxb3+** 53. **Kxb3 Kd6** 54. **Ka4 Kxd5** 55. **Kxa5 Ke4** 56. **Kb4 Kf4** 57. **Kc3 Kg3** 58. **Kd2 Kxg2** 59. **Ke3 Kg3** 60. **h4 Kg4** 61. **Kf2 Kf4** 62. **Kg2 Kg4** 63. **Kf2 Kxh4** 64. **Kf3 Kh3** 65. **Kf4 Kh4** 66. **Kf3 Kg5** 67. **Kg3 h4+** 68. **Kh3 Kh5** 69. **Kg2 Kg4** 70. **Kh2**

Hi Jonathan.

Only just read this. Am going to try and cancel my game tonight as I am feeling rather under the weather. Am just trying to get in touch with David Elsey but there's no-one there at the club yet, apparently. I did begin a small chess group at another library which was going rather well until the snitches got there. I understand you and David have just started one at ours.

I can't breed

Dear Mari (Mrs V-allgreen),

Thank you for agreeing to see us at our local branch. My mum is finding it very hard to get around town now, and a journey all the way into Norwich would leave her very tired and unwell. She will be 84 years old in a few weeks' time.

Prior to our meeting on 14th January (2020) I would like to mention, on behalf of my mother, a few important disclosures, which I think will help us all. I quite understand if you would like to see my mum on her own for a while at first. I think you will probably ignore me.

I have been my mother's full-time Carer for a few years now. I am the only person who looks after her on a twenty-four-hour basis and we live at the same abode. She is becoming increasingly frail and forgetful.

We both thought it would benefit us all to come in and talk over her concerns with you, and for her to re-read her Will to see if everything is worded correctly to her satisfaction.

My mum is unable to find a current copy of her Will even though she has looked everywhere. She caught my sister going through one of her drawers looking for it, the last time my younger sister condescended to bless us with her presence. Mum has also confided in me that there were certain aspects of her old Will that she would like to think over.

My mum has made it clear to me that she would like her home shared equally between myself and my sister. There are no other siblings. She has also said that she would like me to be able to go on living there if anything should ever happen to her. I do not have any other place to live and cannot afford to buy my own house, especially with property being so expensive in the area.

My sister Genevieve already has a home of her own and a rich boyfriend. She lives hundreds of miles away, and does very little for my mum. My sister has told me that if anything should ever happen to my mum I would have to leave, and that I could not go on living here at this address, even though I could probably just about afford to run the place.

We would like this matter clarifying if you don't mind. As you can imagine it makes one feel very vulnerable thinking you could at any moment be turfed out onto the street.

Mr President. Is there any truth in the rumour that Hilary has given Bill a needle full of disinfectant to cure his lungs?

SPONSORED CHILD AT CHRISTMAS

By USULI TWELVES | Published: DECEMBER 17, 2019 | Edit

Dear Mr BUNDERCHOOK,

It was very kind of you to sponsor me, even though we have never met.   Thanks to you I will be able to live a decent life, without having to do anything too disgusting in order to eat. I now have a smile on my face and can rest assured that for the rest of my life I will be blissfully happy.

INNOCENTS FOREVER!

Pete's wife Linda

By USULI TWELVES | Published: DECEMBER 17, 2019 | Edit

Called me "Andrew…" Dead give-away!

AMNESTY INTERNATIONAL

By USULI TWELVES | Published: DECEMBER 17, 2019 | Edit

Come on you racist scum. Take another sixty. What are you complaining at?

Your two dollars will provide clean drinking water for a whole year!

Cor, its all go. the days seem to just shoot by. it gets dark before I get out of bed sometimes… 😊 With regards to the Santa. I just need a red coat and a white beard and moustache, and of course the traditional floppy hat. I love fish. I like chilli and hot food too. I aren't going to tell any of the chess people...I do have a red bag for presents but its not huge. I missed my game last night due to a bad headache. Am feeling a bit better tonight though. I only just got the idea. Then I thought of your big telly. I have a really lovely little film which is for both adults and children. I think they would love it, or at least like it. Its based on a British legend, but I would like to keep it a secret. I just thought we could watch it all together perhaps, if I brought a bottle of wine across one night. Its up to you when. A late afternoon or evening...!

Hi Ruta,

I have a feeling you are out there somewhere. My Santa costume is fine, but have my own red pants. have been experimenting with something to make me look like I have white hair on my head under the hat. please don't laugh, well, you can do if you really want to...just thought it would work best if I came to the door with you when it was quite dark so they didn't know it was me. then I could do all the "Ho ho ho!" stuff and give them their presents. do you have a bell I could ring? let me know what time you want me to be there Coming back in the car from the tournament last night Ruta kept calling me darling. I didn't know if she was so used to her husband being next to her. Her father couldn't speak much English, but he was a great chess player. "Labos nakties papa...."
MATAS
EVA
EMA
ROKAS
EROKAS
MOGLE

Virginija...when I kissed you as Santa I felt a warm feeling I've never felt before. Please give me a bit more time to read over your work.

Dirt on Biden is easy to find. just look underneath his shoes.

60

Pack of violent Israeli tourists rape innocent English holiday-maker

By SARIN | Published: DECEMBER 30, 2019 | Edit

No they didn't! SISTERS NEVER LIE.

Two dozen Israeli soldiers accused of raping Arab tourist guide

By SARIN | Published: DECEMBER 31, 2019 | Edit

"It'll never catch on," says Netanyahu. "We need all our best men at home to prevent further incursions into our territory."

Sir Cliff to represent UK in next year's Eurovision

By GODFREY WINKLEBACKER | Published: DECEMBER 31, 2019 | Edit

Demanded by a huge number of adoring fans
A suitable epitaph for the Peter-Pan of pop
Third time lucky we hope!
Sir Cliff reputed to be "ecstatic!"
Never caught with his trousers down in a public toilet

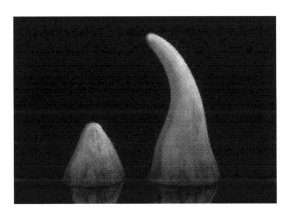

We mourn the death…

By RUMPLESTILTSKIN | Published: JANUARY 1, 2020 | Edit

Of our beloved son; Jeffrey. Father? Brother, tutor, pundit, adviser, coach, sex-guru, who died in such horrible circumstances, through no fault of his own.

Was there ever a better Santa…It was very nice to be able to talk to Valius.

I'll stitch you up better next time!

Second impeachment for Trump...

By GODFREY WINKLEBACKER | Published: JANUARY 4, 2020 | Edit

Democrats are fuming with indignation and disgust because the President did not ask the permission of Congress before suddenly removing one of America's greatest enemies. And thereby take away the element of surprise. Sometimes I think the Clinton's are working for the Arabs.

Drew Gallagher

Just now ·

Thanks for removing my Christmas greeting, you snooping insidious b.stards. So what does that prove?

Calendar girls

By RUMPLESTILTSKIN | Published: JANUARY 1, 2020 | Edit

The Naked Rambler was imprisoned for seven years for doing just the same thing, but don't forget; he is a vandermolen...

Man jailed for having sex in train toilet...

By RUMPLESTILTSKIN | Published: FEBRUARY 11, 2020 | Edit

While his wife listened to all the commotion outside the door.
The 'Victim' said she never enjoyed a single inch of it.
Comments

Hi Heather,

Looking For an Arabian Mate?.....OH, beg yr pardon. I KNOW What you Mean NOW.
I Was at the Feathers just aFter eLeVeN, but they WOULDN'T Let Me iN.
It Was all LocKed up doWNStairs. I told the bLoKe I Had a Friend iN the baNd, but He Said
they didN't Let aNyONe iN aFter eLeVeN o'clocK. Never Heard aNything Like it.
All that Way For NOthiNg. OH, Well, you caN ONLy be PHiLOSOPHicaL about theSe thiNgS.
I WaS SO LOOKiNg ForWard to SurpriSiNg you aNd driNKiNg a NeW Year's toaSt together.
I Hope to See the baNd aNOther tiMe.

Ghislaine Maxwell Scoffing at Law Thanks to 'Serious Dirt' on Powerful People, Former Friend Says

"you've stolen my dreams"

Aren't you ashamed of what you have done?

Why do British teenagers never lie...

By USULI TWELVES | Published: JANUARY 7, 2020 | Edit

Because they love the Jews?

"You're an embarrassment!"

OH, FUCK OFF WILL YOU

HARRIS FOR PRESIDENT

What do you think you'd like to do between now and the day of the trial?

By RUMPLESTILTSKIN | *Published: DECEMBER 20, 2019* | *Edit*

"Thought I'd check out my husband's cock a bit more…"

Grandmother banned from school

By RUMPLESTILTSKIN | *Published: DECEMBER 20, 2019* | *Edit*

A Grand-mother, falsely accused of fraud by the Post office, but with a criminal record, has been banned from being left alone with her grandchild.
"Just about right." Our Local priest.
"Not before time!" Local council chief.
"Suits us just fine." P C Plod

The Chief Inspector

By BIRD DUNG | *Published: DECEMBER 20, 2019* | *Edit*

The Chief Inspector called by the Signalbox today. Its August 1983. He tried to approach me on the blind side.
"We get at least a dozen phone calls every day about you!" he fumed. "When are you going to start behaving like everyone else?!"

Evil criminal arrested eating his Christmas dinner

By BIRD DUNG | *Published: DECEMBER 26, 2019* | *Edit*
Lamb says; cannabis should be legalised.

Personal Physician looking for work...

By USULI TWELVES | Published: DECEMBER 29, 2019 | Edit

off with your clit...

Pretty little Sophie

When I walked in the dining room mum was leading a young woman from the Conservatory.

"Who are you?" I asked.

DEMOCRATS IMPEACH THE PRESIDENT

By PETER SMITH | *Published: DECEMBER 19, 2019* | *Edit*

At long last, the Democrats have impeached the President, in the hope of ending the 'tyranny' of Donald Trump.

"We have impeached him!"

"Such courage in the face of adversity."

"I had to do it for all the angels in heaven."

"It took great moral courage but at last we have succeeded."

"This phone call will go down in history."

"The President broke the law and we don't like it."

"Not even the President should be above the law."

"We had to save mankind from this terrible evil."

"A trial that should be fair, and free from any bias."

"Trump is the enemy of freedom."

"We have done what we had to do to protect this wonderful nation."

"It's the saddest day of our lives…"

"We were always going to do this after the election result."

"Asking for dirt on Biden is like asking whether a pig lives in shit."

Pelosi admits; she's an ass-hole.

'We never asked for Brexit, and we will never let it happen'
"I'd really like to be the first woman to land on Mars. If it's not me, I'd like it to be someone else"
Joe Swindlesome, Pretend you're a liberal, Upper Reichstag, Parliament Road.

'I predict that by the spring of 2020 there will be a severe shortage of arse wipes in most British supermarkets'
Emmanuel Macron, Yellow-vests are sissies, Arrest anyone who goes out of doors, PARIS GHETTO, France.

JiMMy RiddLe

By PETER SMITH | Published: JANUARY 7, 2020 | Edit

Jonathan was smiling a lot at the end of our game. He still wouldn't tell me who gave him the idea to start the library group.
"I don't want loads of kids joining," he said.
He got up again.
"If you are longer than half an hour I'm sending Heather in to look for you!"

The Taverham Vets

By PETER SMITH | Published: JANUARY 7, 2020 | Edit

We had to take Sam to the Vet's today. He's got a poorly eye. The Vet came to talk to me. He needs to have some droplets in twice a day. The Vet thinks he's bumped into something, because he is almost blind. Mum wandered around the room. She didn't like the Vet talking to me.
"He's such a bully!" she shouted.
"Your mum is so sweet," the girl at the counter smiled.
Several women in the queue scowled at me and covered up their breasts.

Donna at the bank

By PETER SMITH | Published: JANUARY 7, 2020 | Edit

I bank with Santander. I have done for years. I went in without my mother today. She needs a lot of support these days.
Donna took me upstairs to discuss the account.
She wasn't smiling any longer

Sydney Smith's Pa

By PETER SMITH | Published: JANUARY 7, 2020 | Edit

Sydney Smith was the old rocker with the huge ginger beard, who used to live next door. He was partly spastic, although tall, walked with great difficulty, and a swinging gait of his legs. He could pull the birds like no-body's business. His father was pale with brown hair. My mum spotted him looking through our letter-box one day when she was having a bath...

Pigs moaning about cuts again

By BIRD DUNG | Published: FEBRUARY 7, 2020 | Edit
Half of them are sat on their arses surfing the net. The other half are too lazy to get out of their panda-cars.

A ridiculous number killed...

By USULI TWELVES | Published: JANUARY 7, 2020 | Edit

In tremendous animal stampede...

Sir Billy Butlin: "The only three things a man needs in life to be happy are power, wealth and women."

The Trump tapes

By SARIN | Published: DECEMBER 18, 2019 | Edit

HYPOCRITES.

There isn't a human being on the planet who hasn't offered something in return for information on a rival.

Death to the Western infidel

By SARIN | Published: JANUARY 5, 2020 | Edit

'We want war with America!'

'We want to be the dominant power in the region.'

The truth is...

By PETER SMITH | Published: FEBRUARY 7, 2020 | Edit

You don't know Jack Shit about me really.

Major News story!

By RUMPLESTILTSKIN | Published: FEBRUARY 7, 2020 | Edit

Phillip Schofield's gay. I could have told you that years ago.

ONe good reaSoN reaSoN WHy yoU SHoULdN't HaVe oN-LiNe aFFairS

UNCLE BLOBBY

Yes it was me! I visited you and found you miserable alone and sad.

Your son sneaked in and watched what you were doing at your computer, on the sofa behind you, covered with a sheet. He kept peering his neck towards the garden, and at you. You kept wafting your hand towards him.

Your daughter wisely left and shut the door after you showed her what you were doing. I have never seen anything so sad in all my life, as you sat there doing things and swigging a bottle of wine...with your hands down your front and elsewhere, bouncing up and down as if it was all a joke.

Your glasses fell off and your trousers were split. You were slumped in your chair and making funny faces now and then, reaching forward to press a key and smile every so often. I thought you were going to slide off...I wasn't sure what you were looking at, or who, but you gave my webcam to someone!

Some of my property had disappeared. I knew the house was being watched.

A strange thing to sign a postcard with your surname...

God I am a noisy git! Wonder it didn't wake you all up slamming the door like that! You were at it again the next day. As a result of phoning you a week later I was given two and a half more years in prison.

You told the Court that the reason you didn't want to appear in person was that I might get 'some kind of sick turn-on at hearing your voice...'

(I don't know if you have ever been inside an institution like that, but you ought to try it if you think it's a funny).

While in prison I used a note-book to write my feelings down and reflect upon my...

I HEARD HER HAVING A HEATED DISCUSSION WITH SOMEONE ON THE PHONE. SHE SHUT THE DOOR. IT WAS JUST AFTER ONE OF HER LONDON TRIPS. "YES, I KNOW YOU'RE HAVING TROUBLE WITH YOUR WIFE AFTER YOUR ARREST. WE ARE FRIENDS! YOU ARE THE BEST FRIEND I HAVE EVER HAD!" SHE HISSED. THEN SHE SAID HER BREAST WERE SORE, AND QUICKLY ADDED, BECAUSE OF MY ROUGHNESS.... HER MOTHER SAID THAT SHE GAVE HER "DOLLOPS" OF MONEY WHENEVER SHE ASKED FOR IT. CROWMARSH BEGAN SMOKING IN THE GARDEN. "SHALL WE GET MARRIED?" SHE ONCE ASKED ME. SHE STARTED TO LEARN THE VIOLIN. A GUY ARRIVED AT HALF-PAST TEN AT NIGHT TO FIX THE PIANO. SHE WANTED HER SON TO HAVE LESSONS. THE GUY APOLOGISED FOR BEING SO LATE AND BEFORE I KNEW IT CROWMARSH WAS INVITING HIM TO STAY THE NIGHT! HER FATHER HAD LAIN DOWN IN FRONT OF THE CAR TO STOP THEM GOING TO CHURCH. SHE TEASED HER SON ABOUT THE SIZE OF HIS EARS. SHE TOLD ME HER MOTHER WAS A BITCH. SHE HID THE WINE BOTTLES FROM HER EX MOTHER-IN-LAW WHO DID MOST OF THE HOUSEWORK STILL. SHE OMITTED TO TELL ROSE ABOUT HER SQUIRTING IN THE KITCHEN.

good and bad omens - April 2005-November 2005
Remove content | Delete | Spam

Spreading the Word of God

By ADUMLA | Published: MARCH 22, 2020 | Edit

Christian evangelists about to export corona virus to isolated Amazon tribes say they are prepared for the worse, but that God is on their side.

"We take people completely as we find them and never judge anyone on the colour of their label"

DEAR DANIEL,

I hope you don't mind me writing to you.

Quite a few years ago I saw a wonderful film called 'Merlin,' with Sam Neill. It was my favourite film for years. I particularly liked the character of young Merlin. There is a scene where he is leaving Ambrosia to go and live with Queen Mab, which is one of the most moving scenes in cinematic history. She's made him a coat to wear, so he doesn't get cold. There are plenty of others as well. I often wondered what had happened to the young actor who played him since he was one of the sweetest most beautiful people in the world. Why had I never heard of him since...I did some research and found out that he was played by an actor called Daniel Brocklebank. I Googled the name, but all it came up with was the vicar on Coronation street; a difficult unhappy man, who looked as if he'd had a very hard life, so I eventually gave up.

A short time ago I was putting some footage of the film on my Face-book page and wanted people to see the young merlin for a change. I found it almost impossible to get any bits with him in it. I looked up his name again, and searched for him on-line. Once again it showed me the vicar from Coronation street.

Then it suddenly dawned on me. I actually cried.

What happened to us Daniel. Did we just get old...?

Love to you always

How do you explain the low number of Covid-19 cases in Germany?

"Sauberere Hände ..."

NAKED FROM THE WAIST DOWN ACTUALLY...

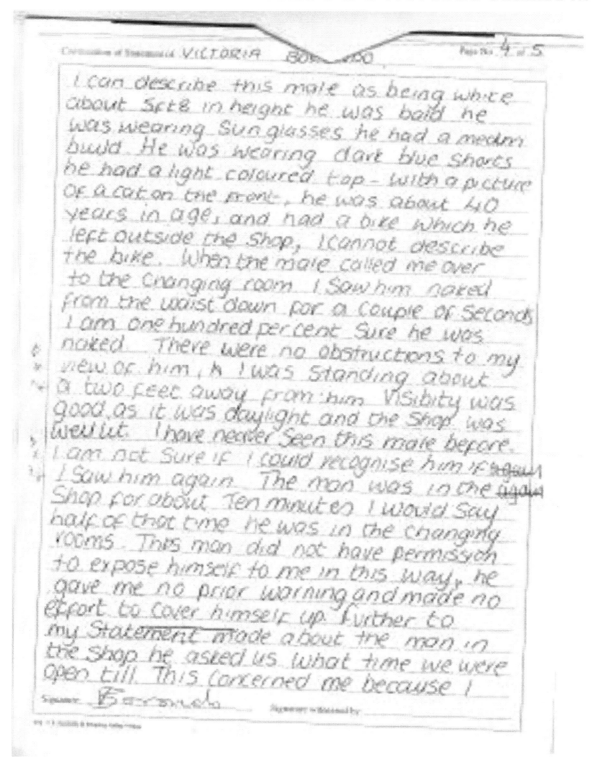

I can describe this male as being white about 5ft8 in height he was bald he was wearing sunglasses he had a medium build. He was wearing dark blue shorts he had a light coloured top - with a picture of a cat on the front, he was about 40 years in age, and had a bike which he left outside the shop, I cannot describe the bike. When the male called me over to the changing room I saw him naked from the waist down for a couple of seconds I am one hundred percent sure he was naked. There were no obstructions to my view of him, & I was standing about a two feet away from him visibility was good, as it was daylight and the shop was well lit. I have never seen this male before. I am not sure if I could recognise him if I saw him again. The man was in the shop for about ten minutes I would say half of that time he was in the changing rooms. This man did not have permission to expose himself to me in this way, he gave me no prior warning and made no effort to cover himself up. Further to my Statement made about the man in the shop he asked us what time we were open till. This concerned me because I

N.B. I did not 'call you over.' You walked to the entrance of the cubicle, where the curtain was slightly ajar, with another pair of trousers, for me to try on, and calmly passed them to me through the gap. I did not give you 'permission to look at me.' This is all that happened. I left the shop soon after. *The night before I decided to do the unthinkable.* For this daring act I was placed on the Sex Offender's Register for the first time in my life, and my whole world turned upside-down. 2005

I'm so sorry Basema.

I went to meet Crowmarsh because she seemed a little lonely. I never felt any physical attraction to her. I just thought she was a bit mad. I sat there every night contemplating my future. I was determined to carry out my plan no matter how loving and caring she was towards me. She must have wondered what I was thinking and why I was behaving so oddly.

I thought she had a nice home and came from a very well-off family, but that they didn't seem to know what was important in life, or to have a clear understanding about how to behave. I was intrigued to learn that her father was a Professor of Literature and had gained first class honours at Oxford alongside some very famous names. I found her children a little strange at first. Why is it so hard to live with anyone? I never had any space. Half the time I was itching to get away.

Her son used to throw things at the door if he couldn't get in our bedroom. Her daughter took me by the hand and led me around for days. We were coming back by ourselves from the fish shop one evening when she asked me who I loved most; her or her mother. I said I loved them both but in different ways. It was an odd carry on. When Benji fell asleep I had to carry him into his own room, but when he woke he only came back again. I walked out on them three times, once at the Phoenicia, in Valetta. On one occasion I watched her run to the door as I stood on the stairs above.

She kept asking me; "Do you think you could love me just a little bit?"

My employer had asked me on Wangari's behalf if I would like to go on holiday with *her*, as she was too shy to ask me herself. We had always got along very well and I felt very comfortable with her, but you know what these big Kenyan girls are like; she was very hairy down below and would have sucked me in and spat me out with those huge bubble-gum lips of hers. I went on holiday with Crowmarsh and the kids out of loyalty to her and to them. One minute she was a religious zealot, then a hounding nymphomaniac. I wasn't sure if I was her companion, carer, or quack. She said I was always coming in late. It was the only time I could get away from work, and anyway, I liked helping her put them to bed and reading their bedtime stories. It was the first and only time I ever felt as if I was part of a family...

I know you loved me my dearest, that you spoke to me in imaginary conversations...and that life in Damascus was very difficult for you...please forgive me for not coming to Cyprus to marry you.

When the day is still

Imagine,
When the earth is still,
I whispered to you, in the darkness,
All alone,
And told you all my thoughts,
Wondering, if things had been a little different, then,
How bright the Sun and Moon would have been,
Before the shadows, like rumbling thunder,
From the void,
The sound of water falling from the sky,
Would we have been the grass and bluebells kissed by rain,
free to roam the castles of the air.

Imagine,
If the day was still,
And I had met you long before that time,
We could have flown above the clouds,
In heaven,
Speaking words of paradise.

Crowmarsh - 2005

I went to meet Crowmarsh because she only lived a few miles away. I never felt any attraction to her. I just thought she was a bit confused. I sat there every night contemplating my future. I was determined to carry out my plan no matter how loving and caring she was towards me. She must have wondered what I was thinking.

I thought she had a nice home and came from a very respectable family, but that they didn't seem to know where they were going or to have any good understanding about the things which matter. I was intrigued to learn that her father was a Professor of Literature and had gained first class honours at Oxford.

I found her children a little strange at first. Why is it so hard to live with anyone? I never had any privacy. Half the time I was itching to get away. Her son used to throw things at the door when he couldn't get into our bedroom. Her daughter took me by the hand and led me around for days. We were coming back from the fish shop one evening when she asked me who I loved most; her or her mother. I said I loved them both, but in different ways. It was an odd carry on. When he fell asleep I had to carry him into his own room, but when he woke he only came back again. I walked out on them three times, once at the Phoenicia, in Valetta. Once I watched her run to the door as I stood on the stairs. She kept asking me; "Do you think you could love me just a little bit?" My employer had asked me on Wangari's behalf if I would like to go on holiday with *her*, as she was too shy to ask me herself. We had always got along very well when we met, and I felt very comfortable in her presence, but you know these big Kenyan girls; she was happy to have a threesome, but would have sucked me in and shat me out without any trouble. I went on holiday with Crowmarsh and the kids out of loyalty to her and for them.

One minute Crowmarsh was a religious zealot, then a hounding nymphomaniac. I wasn't sure if I was her companion, carer, or quack. She said I was always coming in late. It was the only time I could get away, and anyway, I liked helping her put them to bed and reading their bedtime stories. It was the first and only time I ever felt as if I was part of my own family.

life. Prudence said I should be careful about you and anyone else I saw on 'American singles.'

REJECTED

74

for city centre offices, visit.

Three die in swimming pool accident

Hard as Flint

By RUMPLESTILTSKIN | Published: DECEMBER 17, 2019 | Edit

Caroline Flint lost her seat in the recent General election and responded by nailing a long time adversary with a story of filth. She accused Emily Thornberry of calling her electorate "thick." Thornbury denies calling them stupid. She says that she has no alternative but to take legal action to prove that what she said she didn't say. *Jack Shit... More women in Parliament!*

Today's news:

1 As you may have read; William and Harry have had a massive bust up. Kate and Megan are getting on great though. I said, he said, we said.

2 Keith was rushed into A&E after trying to remove his appendix at the back of the cinema.

3 Doctors agree that there are not enough boat people entering the channel.

4 Farley-Hills has changed her name to Mills, but can't remember when.

5 Man arrested on board Ukrainian jet for loose shoe-laces.

'Now then Philip, remember to stay in your own chalet at night.'

MESSAGE TO *AZURITE BLACK*   *'Maybe it was the lamp which obscured* my vision inside your tent. You can sure do cat impressions. How many dildos did you say you had...I would never have guessed you were in Malta.

HEY, BALDY!

The Bald one, Slap-head, Crome-dome, billiard-ball, marsh-mallow monk, coconut eagle, Kojak, Uncle Fester, shears-roach, cue-ball, splat-head, gonk-bag, curlie, bubble-head, bishlong, jizz-master, front-bum, squidly diddly, bucket head, mutton mangler, shronkey, hairy brain, forest-fire, milk dud...

POSTAL BALLOTS

Minnesota man charged for killing woman who honked horn at him

Angelo Borreson was charged after prosecutors accused him of killing a woman named Angela Wynne, who honked her horn at him and told him to hurry up.

Drew Gallagher Are we supposed to like the white honky or not?

Hi Jonathan!

The rook made all the difference, but it was that damned knight which was causing me the problem. I normally try and stop them getting too far forward in the first place. I left the bar quite suddenly. I wasn't getting very good vibes from those two dudes at the bar. Would love to know what they think I've done. Thank you for going through the game with me.

MonStER's FamILY SaY...

By BIRD DUNG | Published: JANUARY 12, 2020 | Edit
We didn't even know he was gay!

HAD A STALK ON

The Temple: Sacred Poems and Private Ejaculations

Dear Virginija,

I hope you are well.
Are you having a good week?
Just to let you know I haven't forgotten you.
Was a bit tired after the weekend. Me and Heather came back with two points each. Not a total wipe-out then.
Had to have a scan on my back yesterday.
The weather is very wet and gloomy but at least its warm and cosy indoors.

Hi Heather!

Great to hear from you, and your funny sense of humour.

I don't mind the rain and gloomy weather if I don't have to go out in it, and even then it can be fun on your bike.

But only if its a short journey.

I felt some numbness in my leg. The Senior Doctor over-ruled her junior who thought it could be my knee pressing on a nerve, and sent me for the MRI. I haven't heard anything yet. The numbness isn't there at the moment.

I am more worried about my fatigue headaches, and pains in my head sometimes.

By the time you read this you will have played the hugely popular 'Mr Paul Badger...'

I wonder if I should have told Steve he was the most hated man in Norfolk. I've heard rumours about why they left to form the Aylsham club.

How was Keith this week?

I make a lot of silly mistakes and errors of judgement when I am tired like that, sometimes.

I got into a deep sleep, but was still tired somehow. But you can't spend the whole day in bed. There are too many things to do! Went for a meal with Lu Si. The only thing she told the truth about was her name.

Hope you won, or at least, did not give away your Queen for nothing!

VIRGINIJA!

So nice to hear from you.

It is getting dark early now, but I don't mind if I am warm and cosy.

Its not been a bad week here either. Life has its ups-and-downs,

but we are getting on quite well at the moment.

Your father is very lucky to have so many good children.

My mum is in bed now. I have just taken her supper and fed the rabbit.

I used to be quite proud of myself when I was younger...

I look forward to giving you some more English grammar lessons soon.

I know the correct way to write but sometimes I take short cuts.

This is me when I was younger.

Even people whose partners are pigs know what c.nts they are

Counter girl

By SARIN | *Published: MARCH 13, 2020* | *Edit*

Called in the bank today.
"'Where is everyone?"
No response.
Paid in my cheque.
"Is there anything else you'd like us to do today?"
"Like what...?"

79

Oil lamps and candles

Oil lamps and candles,
smoulder on our Sunday round,
Whenever there is sun-shine,
Sailing from the hills.

Can you still remember,
The days we talked together,
You were draped in orange,
And I was dressed in brown.

Along the road to Martin's,
Sneered at and a laughing-stock,
But I was proud to think you were,
My sweetheart and my one true love.

PUNISHMENT FOR YOUR LACK OF FAITH

What makes a wizard?

- THE ABILITY TO BE IN MORE THAN ONE PLACE AT THE SAME TIME
- THE ABILITY TO COMMUNICATE WITH THE HIGHER FORCES AND SPIRITS
- THE POSSESSION OF A FAMILIAR OR ANIMAL GUIDE
- THE ABILITY TO FEEL THE THOUGHTS AND FEELINGS OF OTHERS ACROSS EVERY SPACE AND TIME
- THE ABILITY TO TAP INTO THE UNIVERSAL MIND
- THE ABILITY TO SEE THINGS BEFORE THEY HAPPEN
- THE ABILITY TO REGENERATE AND TRANSFORM ONE'S SELF

Cambridgeshire Rapid-play tournament

Attended the chess tournament with Heather and Steve at the weekend. A few familiar faces and a few new ones. Both me and Heather came back with two points each: more than I was counting on. I played young Caitlynn in the first round. A girl with an angelic face just back from South Africa, who was a killer on the chess-board. She played well and was close to victory, but I mashed her in the end game. Just as I was moving in with my two queens she raised her hand to claim I had made, not for the first time in my life, an 'illegal move.' I played fat greasy Derek in the next round. He'd been ear-wigging all my conversations before we started, and then proceeded to wipe me off the board in the middle game. I blundered my rook in the next game and resigned. In the following game little Hassam accused me of trying to employ 'Scholar's mate' against him. He offered me a draw when he could have won. Then I played David, who had beaten Heather in the previous match. After the game he followed me round asking whether he should have given me his bishop. His knowledge on Spurs was highly impressive. David asked me how old I was. I told him I was 23. He said I looked about 50. I'll settle for that!

'It's a very nice picture, but we can't possibly put it in due to your bad name around town'

GAY GORDON: JUST PAYLSHAM MAGAZINE.

ROUTA

I was just going to write to you tonight! I thought it had been too long since we shared our thoughts…We should get together some time for a game of strip poker.
I am sorry you were poorly. It happens to us all sometimes, even the strong.
I wonder if you had some kind of virus, or perhaps you were missing me.
You spent eight hours in custody. What did you do wrong?
Everything is expensive these days, except love.

Kay Burley: "Does Boris Johnson have a problem with women?"

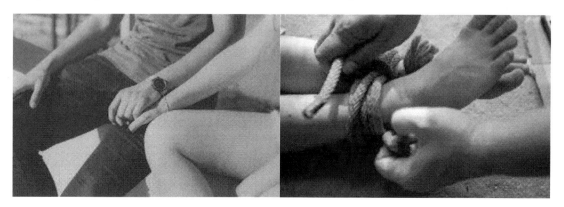

Comments

The closure of some isolated Yorkshire village schools...

THE COME BACK KID

"Swinson for Prime Minister. She'd do well to expose her cleavage."
Field Marshal Gert Mart Rausch, Fide Master, BERLIN.

"Swinson for Outer Space. It would suit her down to the ground!"
His Excellency Motto von Bismarck, Brandenburg gay, TENNIS RACKET.

DEATH THREATS TO POLITICIANS JUST NOT RIGHT

PIG TAKES HOLIDAY ABROAD AT THE TAX-PAYERS' EXPENSE

It's me!

You never asked me about the ending to that dream...?
Anyway, whoever it was replied almost at once "I know you do."
And here's something even funnier.
I was going to tell you some time ago, but please keep it a secret.
I have been feeling a bit poorly the last few days.
I just can't keep things to myself, well, some times I do.
That time I saw Virginija walking towards us at the side of
Cromer church. I thought two things:
1 Why is that nice woman smiling at us.
2 I might marry her one day.
There! I told you it was funny.

EMILY SPANKHURST

BARMY COTTAGE,
LEAKER ROW,
CANARY TOWN.

Dear Surgery,

Thank you for seeing my mother and me together yesterday and for the kind considerate way in which the doctor dealt with her. I made the appointment because of the deterioration in my mum's behaviour during the last year in particular. She is consistently losing things, hiding things and getting very annoyed when it happens. She often blames me for it. Quite apart from destroying the carpet with bleach and toilet cleaner, objects are often left scattered in odd locations throughout the home. Although she did get the day and month correct when the doctor asked, she often makes serious errors. She is always fiddling with things and has broken several appliances throughout the house. If I clean her room she goes and empties cat food all over it.
Although the Doctor stressed looking at her memory, isn't there another diagnosis of 'dementia,' or some kind of *obsessive personality disorder* going on here? My mother deflected the Doctor's enquiry into her awareness by talking about her shoulder.
I thank you for your help and continue to look after my mum to the best of my ability even though I am often poorly myself with headache, fatigue and persistent insomnia.

Yours Sincerely,
BLUNDERBUSS
(for the Little Shitzah)

THE JEW OF MALTA

'As for those Samnites and the men of Uz
That bought my Spanish oils and wines of Greece,
Here have I pursed their paltry silverlings.
Fie, what a trouble tis to count this trash!
Well fare the Arabians, who so richly pay
The things they traffic for with wedge of gold,
Whereof a man may easily in a day
Tell that which may maintain him all his life.
The needy groom, that never fingered groat
Would make a miracle of thus much coin,
But he whose steel barred coffers are crammed full,
And all his lifetime hath been tired
Wearying his fingers ends with telling it,
Would in his age be loath to labor so,
And for a pound to sweat himself to death.
Give me the merchants of the Indian mines
That trade in metal of the purest mold,
The wealthy Moor, that in the eastern rocks
Without control can pick his riches up
And in his house heap pearl like pebblestones,
Receive them free and sell them by the weight,
Bags of fiery opals, sapphires, amethysts,
Jacinths, hard topaz, grass green emeralds,
Beauteous rubies, sparkling diamonds,
And seldseen costly stones of so great price
As one of them, indifferently rated
And of a carat of this quantity,
May serve in peril of calamity
To ransom great kings from captivity.'

85

Trump cannot afford to lose such an ally. He could be accused of naivety, by talking so openly on a line which was bound to be bugged, but then he is used to getting things done. But wait a moment. How many people, including Joe Biden, and many other Politicians and businessmen, have not offered an incentive for information on one of their rivals, or an edge which would give them some advantage? Almost no-one. I bet Pelosi almost fell of her chair with glee. The Democrats have been waiting for something like this for years. The best thing would be to come clean about the entire conversation. Its hard for a President to admit a mistake because it also reflects on his other decisions. He may even end up having to apologise to Joe Biden or give up being so pragmatic. In Roman times you simply assassinated your rivals.

THREE LITTLE ROOMS

Three rooms,
At the top of the house,
On the run-down hill,
Just outside Cromer:
One for Julius and Ruta,
Because they are married,
One for young Ruta and her mother,
And one for Rokas, Erikas and Migle.

But what if I am wrong?

One room for Virginija, Valius and Ruta.
One for young Ruta and laughing Migle,
And one for Rokas and Erikas.

What if I am wrong?
One room for Valius and young Ruta,
One for Virginija and old Ruta,
And one for Erikas, Rokas and Migle…

Dear Andy

Thanks for your missive and kind words.

I'm still feeling a bit dazed and had a weird visual aberration this afternoon. I've had them before, many years ago, but rarely; had a milder one a few weeks ago but hadn't had one for years before that. They were eventually diagnosed years ago as being "Classical" migraine! Have you ever heard of a visual migraine whereby you don't get pain or sickness? But this is like the Aura that some sufferers get, though without the follow-up. I think today's was the worst I've ever had, as it completely blotted out the focal part of my vision in both eyes, though I still had some peripheral vision. It lasted about twenty minutes and has left me feeling pretty washed out. I couldn't see the screen or the newspaper, so decided to ring my sister until it went away! Good job I wasn't driving, I'd've had to stop immediately.

It is very strange how it is in both eyes, naturally one shuts one eye and then the other to test which eye is affected – the answer is both. Of course, it isn't actually in one's eyes, but in the brain ... Shut both eyes, it's still there, a piercingly bright spot to begin with, then it spreads out but becomes a bit more diffused. There were a lot of bright colours over to the right-hand side, but the main part was central. When I put up my hand and tried to look at it, parts of it disappeared completely, as did what I was trying to read. I wonder whether it's connected with my tumble on Tuesday.

Dear Heather,

I feel sorry for you. You can only do what you think is best. Did Keith ever apologise or try to explain why he took off his clothes at the tournament to paddle in the lake? He reminds me a bit of an old friend. I still think Jonathan is beatable. I was winning against him the last time we played when he offered me a draw. Think his grade is about 130. I am 39 in Standard,
My first ever grading! Jonathan is one of the most careful people I have ever played against. He executes everything with a mathematical precision. I am an emotional player. I play with my heart (and sometimes with my head!) ...Harry lost against Matt. I saw him outside.
When I came down a woman was stood at the other side of the bar staring at me. When I went out for my bike her and another bloke were stood next to it.
I played someone on Chess.com today who was a much higher grade than me but they kept deliberately making mistakes and letting me win.
I knew what they were up to, so I deliberately offered them my Queen for nothing (knowing I could get another) but they refused to take it.
I think it could be the Plebs playing games again.

Catch you soon.

'Cleaner water in Africa will mean more boat people for you'
Colin Coastguard Skupper, Thames Estuary Welcome Committee, Free-health-service-pass, London-on-the-Streets.

'I can see it now: an Africa full of high-rise blocks and industrial plants with a population consuming every last grain of water on the planet'
Doctor Florence Bowler, has-an-eye-for-the-men, CHANGE YOUR DOOR TAG AMY, Norfolk.

Hi Andy

You sound defensive. Is there something I should know about you? I did not go to the contest as Virginia and my husband were working on Saturdays I had to stay with my children. And Rokas had a football match on that day. So I missed it. Children were happy that mummy stayed at home.

The time flies and nearly Christmas. Erikas is going on a trip for two days next week with a sleepover, it's his first time. it's always scary for mom. I worry how he will get on. When I was growing up I was very independent, My parents let me to go to Russia on my own to visit my friend and stay with her family for a week. I went by train.

When I went to school, I played chess in a club and we used to play in different towns so we had to stay in some places for 3 or 4 days. it was happy days when we did not have to spend a penny. The government paid for everything: travel expenses, food and accommodation. During half terms and holidays, they gave us vouchers to have a meal in the canteen if we went to a chess club. I loved all the trips. it was a good fun.

I remembered once we stayed in a hotel. And we went to bed very late. Next morning, my coach woke me up but I could not understand how did he get into my room, the doors were locked. Later he told me that he was knocking on my door and I did not opened the doors, he went to reception and asked them to open the room. I slept like a log and did not hear anything. Good night. sleep tight

Ruta

Hi Heather!

Just finished a long letter. It takes time to get the exact wording right, even when you read it over several times.
Its been a quiet day out here in Aylsham. Have been out on my bike twice. I like any excuse to go for a pedal.
My grade last night on Chess.com was 999. I don't know whether to just leave it like that. I could get over 1000 but a lot of my games have crashed, or, like last night, I get one point for beating an opponent ranked hundreds of points above me.
I have played Stephen before and he is really very good. Well played beating Trevor. He's another canny opponent.
I have yet to try this sheep game.
I hope you are well, cosy and warm in your little nest at number 48.
Hope to see you soon!

Love from Andy xxx

15 October 2019

Dear Friend,

I hope you don't mind me writing to you about my experiences at the local Quaker church, which I attended for a few months last year and into this. I had thought about writing to you before. I eventually decided that something needed to be said.

It's about a year ago, when I had just broken up with my long-term partner, that I met a member of the church quite randomly in town, who invited me along to the Centre. I was really just looking to spend a quiet restful hour each week in spiritual contemplation, and this is what I did, for a few months at least. I thought it might help to get me on the right path again, to have a fresh start and to make some new associates in the area.

I was made very welcome, and invited to a lot of barbecues and social get-togethers. One of the church elders tried to coax me along to some week-end development groups. I was treated with great respect and developed a lot of meaningful relationships with people there. I had been brought up a Roman Catholic, but had never been to a Quaker meeting before, and was intrigued to learn more about it. I got along well with everyone, even though I was a lot different to most of them. I'm a former Art student. I think they saw me as someone who could eventually take on some responsibility and become a full and active member of the congregation. While I was there, I behaved impeccably, was polite and considerate to everyone.

In the past I have worked as an Instructor in Occupational therapy, I've been a Signalman and Samaritan. In the last few years I had the pleasure of putting some books together. They are mainly short stories, political and social satire, and poetry. A bit on the zany side. Some of my poetry has been on the BBC.

Some of the members bought my books at a book-signing day in the town hall.

In my biography I confessed that I had once been in prison a long time ago after getting involved with the wrong person and thinking about ending my own life.

On receiving these disclosures all the people at the church suddenly became very cold and distant. I could tell that stories about me had been spread around the whole group of friends. Some of the members even took my books round to the local Vicar, because they thought I had mentioned him. The Vicar was once a close friend of my mother. Quaker friends, who I had happily chatted to over coffee on a Sunday morning ignored me or stared at me with horror and alarm. One of the church helpers, with the full support of one of the elders, tracked down my Face-book page, and began posting derogatory remarks on there.

I got into trouble, nearly eleven years ago, for contacting my ex-partner, when I was very depressed. I was charged with phone contact only; breaking a restraining order not to contact her. One land-line call in which I tried to apologise for a serious misunderstanding, and one disputed text-message. I was never charged with a sexual offence, or anything violent. I was not malicious in any way. This was a partner I had not wanted, even when we lived together.

While in prison I found that the Quakers were the only honest decent people to talk to in the whole establishment. My health suffered and my life was destroyed. They gave me hope that one day I could re-build my life and have something to live for in the future.

I was called into the branch by a very angry and red-faced, Mr Blob Wardman, a church elder at Aylsham. He admitted that he had been doing some digging on me for months, and wanted me to sign a document to say I was a 'Sex-offender,' and that I would agree to regular monitoring by himself and other elders at the church. He had also been talking to the police about me and other members of the Authorities.

I told him that I had once admitted an offence of exposure thirty years ago on a train, but that I had not been charged with any thing sexual against my ex-girlfriend. The police had tried to link these two incidents together even though they had nothing to do with each other. I said it was over and done with thirty years ago and that I was sick of hearing about it. I freely admit to not being a goody-two-shoes, and have done some very silly things in my life. I also told the church elders who were interviewing me that I was fed up of being harassed by the police, but they simply did not want to know. They were very robust in their defence of the police, even though I knew the police had lied on more than once occasion and were quite capable of deception. I told them that I was not a Sex-offender and did not want to be treated like one. Only one of the ladies, Vicky, stood up for me. She said I didn't come across as bad person at all, or a threat to anyone.

Mr Wardman had re-searched a very one sided and biased story about me, which had appeared at the time. I told him that I completely disagreed with the assumptions made in the article and of the way I was portrayed in the media. I told him that I had several excellent references from Professor friends in Oxford where I had lived and worked completely refuting what was said about me. He simply laughed. I asked him not to believe everything he read, but he quoted back pieces from the suspicious article. I felt as if I was between a rock and a hard place. I was extremely upset throughout the whole meeting, which anyone there could vouch for.

The Blab told me that I was "only making excuses for my behaviour" when I wrote an article for the Eastern Daily Press about how I had suffered at the hands of my father as a little boy and about some of the things which had happened to me. I wanted people to be able to read a more balanced and truthful picture of me. He also wanted to know why I had not included the exposure in my biography, and why I had not told everyone about a washing line found in my holiday home which the police said could have been used to tie around my girlfriend's neck. I told him I was trying to explain what had happened as best I could, without avoiding any guilt, not making over-simplified 'excuses,' and could not include every little detail in the article, even though I might have wanted to.

It was implied that all the information gathered about me during my supervision at the branch would be handed over to the Authorities, which surely reflects the prejudice of certain members.

The Elderman said I was 'dangerous,' and needed to be supervised. I said I was not.

I felt that this was just a smoke-screen to get rid of me, and of continuing my ordeal. I felt extremely stressed and that there was no other option but for me to go home and never to go back. Things could never be the same there again. It all began to feel like a bit of a sham.

'Sue' continued to send me church bulletins and invite me back but I decided not to return due to their intention of permanently 'labelling' me as something I never want to be. I hold no grudges against anyone there. If I have served my purpose then they may have learnt *something* from our encounter. I am at present looking after my mum who is not very well.

I'm not pretending to be perfect, or that I have never done some very foolish things in my life. I hope my writing to you may be beneficial, in some small way. If it is, then we will all be a little wiser, even though I fully expect you to take the side of the flock.

I really just wanted you to know about what happened, even though you will not take sides...

Yours Sincerely,

On peace and friendship

CAMPAIGN TO HAVE MORE DANGEROUS PSYCHOPATHS LIVING IN SOCIETY

British Maternity group 1956

I was half asleep and didn't see you. A pretty hopeless night trying to get to sleep.
Had to do a big shop and take her out. Just wanted to get it done and get back home.
My sister coming on Monday.
Rokas kept saying: "You're going in the wrong door Andy!"
I suppose I like trying to beat the door, and anyway, what's wrong with that.
You have lost some weight, I think.

Settings

Andy Amis

I am up late and the weather is so bad for tomorrow, but I am firmly committed to Tona's with you this Saturday!

John Wickham's a nice bloke, but very strait-laced. All you have to do is acquire a 'reputation,' and people will instantly turn on you.

People can be very intolerant of anyone a bit whacky or different. I hope you are alright now.

Lost my game against Jonathan tonight, but it was always going to be difficult. Had a chat with Harry who was playing Matt.

I took them all up a huge plate of free sandwiches which had been given to me by the bar staff. Had the builder here to look at the garage door. Car in on Thursday for service.

Mum has developed a fetish for ice-cream which is driving me mad. She raids the freezer and won't eat the meal I have made her.

That's all for now.

Hi Andy and thanks for that. I hope all is well with you? I'm very tired today but otherwise OK.

Ah, it's Friday coming that we are going to Southwold, but I have been before to Charles's house there.

You'll be most welcome at the New Year's Eve gig, we do all the traditional stuff, bongs of Big Ben, *Auld Lang Syne,* *The Hokey Cokey, Knees Up Mother Brown* ... I thank you for your most philosophical reassurance on last night's débâcle. I shall try to adopt your sensible and mature attitude. I think I'm quite laid-back on most things, but not when it comes to my job! We had a worse débâcle this afternoon; taking Keith to the Norfolk County Championships was a grave error of judgement on my part. I was in the foyer chatting with FM Martin Walker, who was leading the competition to be Norfolk County Champion, though it was not yet in the bag as several other games that could affect the result had still to finish. Keith had gone into the playing room and had been watching the games. Then John Wickham (the Arbiter) came flying out, saying to me:

"I've had to ask Keith to leave but he is refusing to go!"

I said: "Why, what has he done?" John wouldn't say but said: "Please don't ever bring him again to any event where I am Arbiter."

I said I would take Keith back to his home, and did so. He wouldn't say anything about whatever it was that had happened. Thus I never found out whether Martin had won; but it was looking good when we left. I was so disappointed to miss what I'd come to see, and upset about Keith. There were people there with whom I needed to speak, but didn't get the chance as they were still playing. At least I got to arrange my lift to Bury St Edmunds with Bodo, though since I shall have to drive halfway there to Bodo's and back, it is only really half a lift ...

No, Ruta didn't appear.

I'm glad you've had a good day and got some chores done. Heck hasn't it rained! There was a big flood in front of the venue, Keith took off his socks and shoes and waded across!

Yes, see you Saturday, if not before.

Love from Heather x

Virginija   Care Certificate 9

- ✓ Start sentences with a capital letter and end with a full-stop.
- ✓ Try not to leave any gaps.
- ✓ Keep sentences flowing on the same line.

Dementia....*They could have...*

Negative attitude

Thinking that someone with a learning disability, or who is suffering from a mental illness, is somehow inferior to everyone else.

Impacts

The way people are treated affects their well-being and self-esteem. If they are treated badly or insensitively, they are more likely to become anti-social, distressed and unhappy.

Positive change

Listening carefully and patiently to the person and hearing their needs without forcing my views on them.

Impact

In the end this will help to make them happier more rounded individuals. It will help to give them encouragement to develop new skills and ways of coping.

HUNTER BIDEN

Ukrainian people smuggler and Russian agent.

WE NO LONGER BELIEVE IN HANGING OR SHOVING MATCHSTICKS BEHIND YOUR FINGERNAILS. WE HAVE FOUND NEW WAYS OF GETTING RID OF YOU AND OF TORTURING YOU TO DEATH.

NHS Heroes: **a toxic atmosphere of fear.**

Hi Virginija,

Yes. I finished that paper about child-care but when I sent it to you all my changes had disappeared. Maybe it is tied to your e-mail or something.

You had already sent it off anyway. When will you know if the work you sent in was alright..?

Apparently the children had not had any food that night I was there. They were complaining about being hungry or something.

You sent me a message that you were starting a Health and Safety paper. I only just got the message today, so where it's been for the last three days...

If you would like me to read it over or help you with it in any way please send me a copy.

I actually enjoy doing this sort of study.

Its cold and dark outside now.

I hope you've had a good week.

Best Wishes,

Andy *Theydon'tknowJackShitaboutme*

BILES MOST DECORATED GYMNAST IN HISTORY

```
see     what you probably don't realise
soon as you say anything to mum or she doesn't get her own way
when I asked her to let me put a plate over her stew just now for instance
she can get very aggressive    and always comes out with:
you deserve to be in prison
I will tell them what you're like
I never asked you to come here
You won't get out this time...
don't know who's the worse bitch her or Aunty Jenny
what an ignorant pair...
```

BOUNDERCHOOK (1352) vs. **Fotomayes** U.S.A. (1941) 1-0

Chess.com: Live Chess: 2020.10.06 (A Rapid-play game scheduled for 10 minutes, but lasting 7.52)

1. **d4 d5**2. **e4 dxe4**3. **Nc3 f5**4. **f3 Nf6**5. **h3 Nc6**6. **Bb5 Qd7**7. **Be3 a6**8. **Bxc6 Qxc6**9. **Qe2 Be6**10. **O-O-O Bc4**11. **Qf2 e6**12. **Nge2 Bb4**13. **a3 Ba5**14. **d5 exd5**15. **Nf4 Bxc3**16. **bxc3 Qa4**17. **Kd2 Qxa3**18. **Ke1 Qxc3+**19. **Bd2 Qxc2**20. **fxe4 Nxe4**21. **Qd4 O-O-O**22. **Ne6 Rde8**23. **Nxg7 Ng3+**24. **Kf2 Re2+**25. **Kxg3 Qb3+**26. **Kh2 Re4**27. **Qf6 Be2**28. **Nxf5 Bxd1**29. **Qxh8+ Kd7**30. **Qxh7+ Kc6**31. **Qg6+ Kc5**32. **Qg7 Kb6**33. **Be3+ c5**34. **Qf6+ Kb5**35. **Nd6+ Kb6**36. **Nxe4+ Kb5**37. **Nxc5 Qc4**38. **Rxd1 Qe2**39. **Rb1+ Kc4**40. **Qd4#**

HIYA!

I hope you are feeling fine, and are having a good week.

I hope everyone at home is well.

Did you ever find out what was wrong with you that day,

when you were poorly driving back from King's Lynn?

Virginija gave me a paper to help her with, but when I

sent it back, first of all my alterations had disappeared

from my original. Don't know why it did that. And...

she had already sent it in by then....! Oh well. I am

waiting to hear from her about some more.

She is a very sociable person isn't she. Her phone

was always ringing.

I am a bit of a stick in the mud sometimes. I have

to practically force myself to go out and socialise.

My mum has been a bit difficult today. I am just

about to go out and see to the rabbit.

I would like to give you some more English lessons,

I just haven't got round to it yet. I've been busy with

everyday things, and trying to run an ad campaign

for some of my books.

Look forward to hearing from you.

'Strength is persevering, when you want to give in. Courage is acting bravely, in the face of adversity. Wisdom is seeing things in a frank and honest way' Mojo Ming, Chief Political pundit, British television, PEEKING.

'My sister always was good at picking up black men' 'Do you know anything at all about her past you lonely old Paddy?' V. Isle de Grader, Ammunition from PAKISTAN. Irish Main-land.

one other little thing   really not your bag

the ACT Centre where mum goes

the girls are very nice but one of them keeps

giving mum a lot of attention

Pete Tubby's wife

she;

1 criticized me for wearing my sun-glasses in-doors
2 said I shouldn't be driving with my wing-mirrors in

THE ARTFUL DODGER TRAM-WORK

STILL CAN'T GET OVER THAT KID ACCUSING ME OF TRYING 'SCHOLAR'S MATE' ON HIM IN WHITTLESFORD. I THINK YOU ARE GRADUALLY WEARING BOSTIK DOWN. I BELIEVE HE IS CLOSE TO CRACKING!!
HAD A STRANGE ONE THIS MORNING..WAS IN MANCHESTER OR SOMEWHERE WEARING DIFFERENT CLOTHES AND LOOKING FOR THE RAILWAY STATION. I THOUGHT ABOUT ASKING SOMEONE, BUT THEN MY FORGOTTEN MAGIC POWERS CAME TO THE RESCUE. USING THE POWER OF MY MIND I ZOOMED UP INTO THE AIR SO I COULD SEE OVER THE TOPS OF THE BUILDINGS (IN GREAT DETAIL)...THEN I SOARED EVEN HIGHER, AND WAS ABLE TO SEE EVEN FURTHER AFIELD AROUND THE CITY.
AM USUALLY GOOD ON THE WILL-POWER SIDE BUT SOME BAD HABITS ARE HARD TO BREAK. I HATE JABS OF ANY KIND OR ANYTHING MEDICAL. I MIGHT JUST GIVE IT A MISS IN THE MORNING, BUT PLEASE SEND MY BEST WISHES TO EVERYONE. I WILL BE BACK SOON AND WILL SEE YOU ON MONDAY ANYWAY. FUNNILY ENUFF I WAS LOOKING THROUGH MY OWN MATCHES EARLIER AND SAW YOU WERE DOWN TO PLAY JOHN. I'M NOT BEING FUNNY BUT IF YOU DO BEAT HIM, WHICH YOU HAVE EVERY LIKELIHOOD OF DOING OF COURSE, ESPECIALLY IF YOU DON'T BLUNDER YOUR QUEEN IN THE FIRST FEW MOVES, I PROMISE TO EAT ONE OF MY HATS FOR BREAKFAST.

GOOD LUCK WITH THE CAT.

LOVE AS ALWAYS XXX

What attacked a 13-foot great white shark pulled from the ocean? Ocean researchers pulled a 13-foot great white shark from the sea - which had bite marks from an even bigger predator. The giant shark, named Vinny by researchers, was caught off the coast of Nova Scotia earlier this month.

WELL, I HAD JUST SIGNED IN, WHEN YOUR MESSAGE CAME.   CHILDREN TAKE UP A LOT OF YOUR TIME AND ENERGY, BUT THEY WILL BE GROWN UP BEFORE YOU KNOW IT.   REMEMBER THEM THIS WAY. THESE ARE THE BEST TIMES OF YOUR LIFE. I THINK YOU ARE A GREAT COOK. REMEMBER THE BAKEWELL TART YOU MADE... A BIT BURNT BUT TASTY INSIDE!   I HAVE BEEN IN TOUCH WITH VIRGINIJA ABOUT HELPING HER SOME MORE. JUST WAITING TO HEAR FROM HER.   I MET HER

OLDER DAUGHTER WHEN I WAS THERE. A SORT OF *BIG TEDDY BEAR*. IN SOME WAYS ITS AN IDEAL SITUATION; THEM GROWING UP TOGETHER, AND FORGING CLOSE RELATIONSHIPS.

THE BOYS DON'T NEED A SISTER NOW, AND IT WILL HELP THEM TO LEARN ABOUT GIRLS. I AM GOING TO SEE WHAT'S IN THE KITCHEN TO EAT FOR SUPPER SOON. DON'T THE DAYS GO BY FAST. DO YOU STILL MISS ME...

Andy

Dear Andy

Many thanks for getting me my card, it was good to see you last night and I was glad to give you your £10 before I spent it on something else! I'm glad you were feeling better once you got there. I think it's usually worth going out, even if you don't feel like it. How many times have you gone out and regretted it later? I think if I still feel bad after half an hour or so, I can always come home – at least I'll have shown my face and people will know I'm still alive ☺

It's better than sitting at home feeling bad, when there is nothing to take your mind off it. Well done against the mighty Bostik, that was a superb victory on your part! So were you White in that game? I didn't really look at any other games whilst I was playing – John Wickham could, of course, afford to do so without risking losing ...Yes, we had a good game, even though it was only ever going to go one way – I was pleased to last 39 moves before he checkmated me. Like all good players, he didn't come out all guns blazing but took time setting up his position, and I did the same. But as I did so, I came out at him rather boldly and probably rashly – I think you have to do that against strong players, otherwise they just creep towards you like a glacier until you have nowhere to go. You might as well have a go at them and make them work for it, rather than sit there getting crushed and having a miserable game. I enjoyed the game and he was kind enough afterwards to go over the game with me and to say I had played well. Yes, I thought I played up to my standard, so I was happy. I didn't make any really crass blunders – nor any illegal moves! Though I haven't yet looked at it on the machine so maybe it will disagree.

I am pleased you are playing in the team against Wymondham, and I know you won't let them down. What board will you be on? Board 3 has White, Board 4 Black ... They are a lovely club at Wymondham, you'll enjoy it. Are you going on your own? Travelling with a team-mate or two is usually better ☺

Well I'm off to the GlassHouse in a while, but first I want to look at my game from last night, and do some puzzles. I did well on my Cubes this morning ☺

Pickering, 1838 - 361 pages

```
When I came back from my match tonight mum had hidden all the controls
my friend said he had seen me in the paper.
when I came back I told mum (she'd been talking to that creep Jack down at
the church this aft)
she said she already knew. I said, then why didn't you tell me?
please tell me why I had to grow up among so many Watsons
on second thoughts...don't bother.
```

```
Dear Kindle/Create,
Could I first of all thank you for all your kind help over the years. Could I also mention
something very important,which I would really like to reach the ears of people high up in the
organisation. When a company like Amazon is very successful, there will always be someone,
namely Governments and the media, who will want to knock them down.  Its partly
jealousy.  Sometimes they use the excuse of 'terrorism,' or child abuse. It gives them a
chance to suppress anything they don't like to hear. We greatly appreciate the opportunity
you have given us to have our voices heard.  In the name of free-speech I sincerely hope that
this long continues. We take great care in the publishing of our work.  A Writer's work
should be challenging. It should test the boundaries without being malicious or harmful.
I hope you will do everything you can to sustain this great enterprise!
The main-stream Writers are all a part of the Establishment.
```

Hi Heather!

I lost my match tonight at the Dons, but the guy I played said I was far better than my grade. He began by asking me a lot of very personal questions, then proceeded to stamp his pieces down each move in a very aggressive manner. oh well. Rupert won his match, even though he was a rook down. Pete drew against Colin Goodchild, although Colin made a slight mistake in the end game. Ann drew as well. They asked me about you.
Maybe Bostik is suffering a slight loss of form. Are you sure he doesn't have a virus...
My mum had hidden all the controls while I was out. She had one.

Hi Heather,

I am just up in the middle of the night to do some 'mashed potato,' to go with the liver, onions and gravy I made earlier. I thought I might as well do it now, then all you had to do was heat it up tomorrow. Were you alright today? Were you a bit tired. You still put me to bed well enuff! The game which really got under my skin was the one where I let you pin my king and bishop. This sort of blunder is caused by laziness and not looking at the board for long enough. I feel a bit sorry for picking on Sally every time, although she is sweet. Are you cross at me for wanting a slow build up before the real battle begins!
I guess there's still a bit of time until the potatoes are done for me to have another game...

V Dajkiri of Lebanon...

It was scheduled for ten minutes but lasted less than one.

1. d4 c5 2. dxc5 e6 3. b4 a5 4. c3 axb4 5. cxb 4 b6 6. Be3 7. Bxc5 Qf6 8. Bxf8 Kxf8 9. Qd6+ Ke8 10. Nc3 Qxc3+ 11. Qd2 Qxa1+ 12. Qd1 Qxd1+ 13. Kxd1 Rxa2 14. e3 Ra1+ 15. Ke2 B a6+ 16. Kf3 Rxf1

Well I've done the rabbit, made mum her supper and watered the flowers am going to try not to have a w today....

'Brexit brings the best out in everyone. Our wonderful human nature will always shine through!'
"Who's laughing now?" Jean-Claude Bonker, Holiday pay, Captain-on-the-Seine, FRENCH REPUBLIC.

**Comments**

What's the best way to get a protester off the roof of a train?

PEOPLE SMUGGLERS

✓ Taking advantage of the:

POOR and tRUStING

BADLY EDUCatED

THE LESS intELLIGEnt

THE BRaVE

PEOPLE LOOKInG FOR a BEttER LIFE...

A terrible tragedy, BUT...

I'm going to stick my neck out here, and say we probably haven't heard the full story yet. I am so fed up of the Authorities controlling what we hear with the complete acquiescence of the press. Okay, the dude looks dodgy and he's got funny eyes, but I'm not going to be one of the people who jump on the band-wagon before I have heard from him. He may just come from what some people regard as a deprived background himself. No-one knowingly leaves 39 people in the back of their truck to die. I do wonder if the amount of money they are alleged to make really is that accurate. There must be a few overheads and a lot of danger involved. High Court Judges get paid a lot more, and that's just for sitting on their arses.

I really must apologise for not being there tonight. I have only just finished doing the teas and its nearly eight o'clock. I haven't felt very well all day. Oh, what a miserable thing I am. I really wanted to be there. No, I wasn't asked to be in this one, although I would like to play for them again and do much better. You did alright. Don't forget what intelligent people you are up against. To come away with anything is a bluddy miracle. My sister is here for three days now. I am lending her the car so she can take mum out wherever she wants to go. I really wish I felt better. Lots I've been through. I keep getting a dull headache and fatigue. Still having a lot of problems sleeping. The doctor thinks I suffer from anxiety. Seems daft doesn't it. Where are the Swallowtails from?

I hope to hear from you soon. It really looks cold and wet out there.

Hello

"I COULD Say YOU WERE HaLF aSLEEP. ROKaS WaS aSKING ME WHat'S WRONG WITH ANDY HE WaLKED tHROUGH tHE WRONG DOOR. AS YOU SEE tHE RULES FOR HIM aRE VERY IMPORtaNt aND HE COULD NOt UNDERStaND HOW COULD YOU USE EXIt DOORS. WE HaD a GREat SHOPPING WITH ROKaS, HE LOVES tO GO WITH ME WHEN ERIKaS Stay at HOME aND WatCH TV. YOU HaVE tO DO SOMEtHING aBOUt INSOMNIa. I WOULD UNDERStaND IF YOU FEEL GREat aND HaVE

LOTS OF ENERGY, BUT YOU FEEL TIRED. LAST FRIDAY WAS MIGLE'S BIRTHDAY. HER BROTHER EDVINAS CAME ON SATURDAY WITH HIS WIFE AND LATER MY BROTHER. OUR HOUSE WAS FULL OF PEOPLE AS ALWAYS. THIS SATURDAY WE ARE ALL TRAVELLING TO LITHUANIA. IT IS MY DAD'S 70'S BIRTHDAY. WE COULD NOT MISS IT AND DECIDED TO HAVE A PARTY TO CELEBRATE."

Ruta

Show original message

Hi Ruta,

What a lovely letter. Yes, was hoping to get in and out of the supermarket without being seen and get back home to bed, but bumping into you was an unexpected pleasure. I quite understand about that. I also believed that rules were paramount. He did make me laugh. The real reason I walk in that door is:

1 to try and beat the door (as I said)

2 because I am too lazy to walk over to the other side, and
3 just to be awkward.

We live in a society where we are always being told what to do.

Rokas likes having you to himself sometimes. That's probably one of the reasons he likes going together. He's really quite soft inside. I am very sociable when I get in a gathering but I also like quiet peaceful times, such as walking in the countryside or just simple dreaming.
I had to pick up my sister at the station today. She is stopping three days with us. I have just finished making tea. Virginija said it was Migle's birthday last week. I haven't got round to doing any more work for her. I like doing it by the way. I am very experienced in the things she is doing. I like testing my mind and trying to help. I wish you all the best on your trip to see your father, a safe journey and lots of fun.
You know the rest!

Love from Andy xxx

Comments

Hi Bruce!

Was sorry to miss the club last night. Family commitments and headache.
I did notice a couple of things about the chap I played in Wymondham for
the Gladiators (great name by the way).
He began by asking me a lot of personal questions, as if he had been
expecting me, and during the game he kept slapping his pieces down in a
very aggressive manner. I thought he must have been doing it to intimidate me.
I had him in a lot of trouble but I held back on castling, which proved to be fatal.
He did say at the end of the game that he thought I was a
lot better than my grade. I don't know his name but he was obviously very
experienced. That was only my second league game for the club.
I would like to do others some time. I am determined to do much better.
Russel Reeve turned up unexpectedly, which meant there were five of us.

David Owen bought you bangers and mash. Not such an old skinflint afterall then.
Done lots of jobs today, but am going off the idea of attending the club. they are warning people to avoid non-essential contact. I will have to play Pete later in the month though. Congratulations on

your great victory! I am wondering about Tona.They are telling people to avoid visiting Care homes, and the like, unless they really have to. I am currently playing in a tournament for Norfolk Knights.

Dear Heather,

Thanks for that! So you only jeer at me because you care about me. I am used to people ganging up against me it's the only way they can win.

I do tend to get a bit more confrontational when I haven't slept. I can't sleep when I do go to bed. I sleep in the most odd way. It feels so different from what it used to be like. Does that make any sense? I would offer some of my own work for you to read, but you might find it too upsetting. Its also very subversive and provocative. What is Dannie's surname again. He did tell me. Its a great title for a book. Nine lives…

I just aren't playing enough competitive games where I can boost me grade. The competition we had at the club against very highly graded didn't help. I can understand why people like to see a high grade next to their name, but it doesn't mean that much to me. The best players may not have any grade at all!

You may disagree...in fact, you probably will.

After leaving you (without my usual hug I have to say) I shot into town, scurrying this way and that, trying to get everything done before they closed, dying to go....leaving my things in the car, and having to hurry across town again, hardly able to walk, and then to get home, and find my driving license is missing from my bag. Most likely it is on the pavement somewhere. This is so typical. On some occasions I have raged against this discrepancy of the mind, only to find whatever I was looking for in my bag the next day.

Hi Heather!

We had a pleasant day....well, after seeing my sis off at the station. I took my mum to the ACT Centre. The girls were very nice. My sis said I was on my own from now on and that she was never coming back. Phew!

BUNDERCHOOK VERSUS CARLSEN

1. **d4 e6** 2. h4 **Qe7** 3. **g3 Qd8** 4. **e3 Bb4+** 5. **c3 Bd6** 6. **Nf3 Qe7** 7. **e4 h5** 8. Bg5 **f6** 9. Bf4 **Bxf4** 10. **gxf4 Nh6** 11. **e5 f5** 12. **Ng5 Ng4** 13. **Be2 b6** 14. **Bf3 c6** 15. Nd2 **b5** 16. c4 **b4** 17. **c5 a5** 18. **Nc4 d5** 19. **Nd6+ Kf8** 20. **Nxc8 Qd8** 21. **Nd6 Na6** 22. **Ngf7 Qd7** 23. **Nxh8 a4** 24. **Ng6+ Kg8** 25. **Bxg4 fxg4** 26. **Qxa4 Qd8** 27. **Nb7 Qb8** 28. **Ne7+ Kf7** 29. **Qxc6 Kxe7** 30. **Qb5 g6** 31. **a3 b3** 32. **O-O Nc7** 33. **Qb4 Ra7** 34. **c6+ Kf7** 35. **Nd6+**

Will you please stop snooping into my account, you brain-dead lame-brained blabber-shites.

Hi Andy and thanks for that.

Yes, it was a nice session, and lovely to see you and to spend pleasant time with our dear friends. Thank you for taking me and bringing me back. Just finished a big heap of three months' scanning and accounts ... I thought it was two months – doesn't time fly K Ha, Pete winning, that's nothing. John Pearl beating me 4:1 last night, his grade is lower than Pete's but he got me time and time again! I wrote to Charles Mutty Smutty to say he should accept the alarm system etc being recommended for him, otherwise we just worry about him. I think Tona is going to give him a good nagging J

I'm very tired tonight and have already cleaned my teeth ready for bed ... Just doing a few more puzzles but I'm failing more and more as I can't really keep my eyes open ...

I'm well, apart from that, thanks, and hope you are, too.

Love from Heather x

Great to hear from you. Bruce is one tough opponent. Matt said his grade was around 150. I am a bit impatient to build up small advantages like they do. I like a fast dangerous game.

Would have liked to see more of Pete's game against the Boss.

Callum makes me laugh. He plays in the true spirit of the game.

I made a joke to Charles about his card, that's all. It was very funny what he wrote inside. A nice man.

American cars driving on the left side of the road

By GODFREY WINKLEBACKER | Published: JANUARY 19, 2020 | Edit

When it should be the right side!

MAVERICK

'WHERE DOES IT SAY MEN MUST BE ARRESTED FOR MAKING A PASS AT A WOMAN?'
H. Wine-stain, Film-buff, Back seat On-your-Tod, NEW YORK PENITENTIARY.

'Every life should have a few crazy moments in it'

Dear Virginija,

There are always problems getting your connection right, I don't know why.

Hi Ruta,

I hope you are well and happy. I played against Fide Master Martin Walker on Saturday with my Polish chess set. He makes me laugh the way he walks. Quick short steps. It was a close fought and epic game in which he just about scraped through, but only by the skin of his teeth...!
The bug keeps coming back on me. I had to play Father Christmas wondering if I would have to rush off to the thunderbox. Have been a bit wobbly all day. Time for one last brew before hitting the sack. Oh, you keep telling me that about Bostik. Have some family business to sort out at the Solicitor tomorrow. Just want to get it done so I can let my hair down…

Grosser Indecency

Yep, my old friend Dave Wright played rhythm guitar and vocals with the Troggs on Wild Thing (Number 1 in the US). 'Love is all around' is another great one by them. He died a few years ago at the age of 64.

What a beautiful voice. I thought it must be you.
Have you heard anything from Sally?
With chess you just have to take your victories with your defeats and treat them both the same...as the old poem goes.
I still have a tendency to rush into things without thinking. partly because of my blasé attitude to life, and also because am trying to bamboozle my opponent with speed.
There are some opponents that give me the creeps on line with their sneaky moves and lightning reflexes...!
It's bluddy cold out there.

How to fill a medieval trebuchet

By SARIN | Published: JANUARY 18, 2020 | Edit

- ➢ with the bodies of plague victims
- ➢ bees or wasps nests
- ➢ the head of a recently captured enemy
- ➢ horse-dung, piss, excrement or holy bibles

With God on your side you were bound to be victorious!

Hi Heather,

Just back from the club, but there was no-one there. The room was in darkness upstairs.
I came back down, only to discover, from Kim at the bar, that it was Sunday, and not Monday. Who in hells name swapped the days around??

Had a pleasant chat with Pip at the bar though, who is a life-long fan of Rory Gallagher and Taste.

I told him about that night you saw them, but could not remember what place it was. I guessed about 1967, on their first ever appearance in England.

GUN CRIME ON THE INCREASE

SOFT AS SHIT

Dear *Anointed One,*

Thank you for your letter. We enjoyed reading your comments about my brother Andrew. They have been instrumental in me seeking an immediate meeting with my mother with a view to having him neutered at the soonest opportunity.

Yours,

In gratitude,

Charles

SPIRITUAL HEALER

Bunderchook

Shock, horror!

By SARIN | *Published: FEBRUARY 16, 2020* | *Edit*

Eighty-year-old man dies of corona virus, and aid agencies plead for billions of dollars to be spent on vaccine.

Michael Muggins

By SARIN | *Published: FEBRUARY 16, 2020* | *Edit*

Dear Darl'n Michael,

Congratulations on your recent marriage to Pain-in-the-butt. There are a lot of very lonely people out there. I hear you are a very 'decent' man.

Good luck to you for the future!

Needle-work Scientist of World-renown

Celebrities a waste of space

By PETER SMITH | Published: FEBRUARY 17, 2020 | Edit

Can't get their own way, and they kick-off.
Okay at giving it out, or laughing at the less-than-perfect.
Petulant, pouting, and greedy.

"LOVEY"

By SARIN | Published: FEBRUARY 17, 2020 | Edit

"You dumb mug, get your mitts off the marbles before I stuff that mud-pipe down your mush - and tell your moll to hand over the mazuma"

"Pin your diapers on"

"Go fly a kite, go stick your thumb up your ass"

"The hotel-sneak used to be my lay"

"He was too far off the track. Strictly section eight"

"I got a Chink ribbed up to get the dope"

"And don't bother to call your house peeper and send him up to the scatter"

"If you're not a waiter, creep"

"Tooting the wrong ringer"

"I've been shatting on my uppers for a couple of months now"

"What's the wire on them?"

Winestain

By RUMPLESTILTSKIN | Published: FEBRUARY 18, 2020 | Edit

Guilty of 'predatory behaviour,' inconsistent with normal human endeavour.

My racist Grand-father

By RUMPLESTILTSKIN | Published: FEBRUARY 18, 2020 | Edit

- ✓ Said the town would be taken over by people coming in from abroad.
- ✓ Insisted he had not fought in two world wars just to give everything to spongers.
- ✓ Swore the National Health Service would be swamped with sprogs.
- ✓ Was brain-washed from an early age by priests working for the Wops.
- ✓ Always walked around with a fag tucked behind his ear.

Crime Prosecution hum-bug

By USULI TWELVES | Published: FEBRUARY 16, 2020 | Edit

- • WE NEVER PROSECUTE ANY VULNERABLE PEOPLE
- • WE DO NOT LISTEN TO RUMOUR OR IDLE SPECULATION
- • OUR DECISIONS ARE ALWAYS COMPLETELY IMPARTIAL
- • WE DO NOT HAVE ANY FRIENDS WORKING FOR THE MET

EVERY VOTE IS COUNTED…

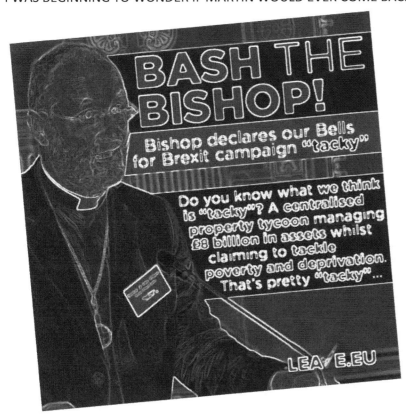

 'If the door was open, I'd still come down the chimney...!'

Write a comment... **too busy bashing hell out of his bell-end...**

"There was a guy on telly who was always getting his cock out in public. Women were screaming their heads off for him to get it out. He said that he could see that some of the white guys had bigger cocks than him, but that the white women still shouted 'more big-black-cock!'"

- Kobe Bryant and the Sexual Assault Case That Was Dropped but Not Forgotten
  A 2003 rape accusation changed how many saw the Lakers star, but it did not change the trajectory of his career.

Observations in space

By SARIN | Published: MAY 9, 2020 | Edit

Due to the rate matter is moving, the passage of light over many millions of years and the space-time continuum, when we observe the farthest galaxies, we could be observing our own beginnings.

•

•

Anthony Joshua says: *Published: MARCH 25, 2021 | Edit*

'You couldn't punch your way out of a paper bag...you over grown piece of cob travelling muck!'

INFORMATION WANTED ON JOE BIDEN

By RUMPLESTILTSKIN | *Published: JANUARY 17, 2020 | Edit*
Including any sordid details about his private life.

Nuclear deal bad for Trump!

By RUMPLESTILTSKIN | *Published: JANUARY 17, 2020 | Edit*
Say Sky News...

Emily Thornberry

By RUMPLESTILTSKIN | *Published: JANUARY 17, 2020 | Edit*
"Based on what is right and what is wrong, we will fight fight fight until the evil Boris is defeated, and a new more fairer society is created."

TRUMP MAKES GREAT PHONE—LINE JOKE...

By USULI TWELVES | *Published: JANUARY 20, 2020 | Edit*
Just goes to show; you shouldn't read anything into things you don't know about.

Comments

WE ALWAYS TELL THE TRUTH

Sepsis kills one in five

By GODFREY WINKLEBACKER | Published: JANUARY 17, 2020 | Edit

"Thank God for that!"

Hassan Rouhani: "death to the Americans. Death to the English!"

Dear Butt,

For the last time of asking, could you please return the car keys. Little Shitzah no longer drives or tries to find the keys. We may need them in the future. If you don't return them I will have to go to the pigs. I am sending you some money and an envelope.

"I only asked her to play with my teddy bare."

Watch-out Harry!

By SARIN | Published: JANUARY 21, 2020 | Edit

You're about to be dumped on from a great height.

Woman accused of racist behaviour…

By GODFREY WINKLEBACKER | Published: JANUARY 25, 2020 | Edit

says: "I'm still married to a black man."

John Bercow 'brutalized' people: even those "lower down the pecking order!"

By PETER SMITH | Published: FEBRUARY 4, 2020 | Edit

Say fellow MP's hoping to scupper his elevation to the Lords.

The old Brock

By PETER SMITH | Published: FEBRUARY 4, 2020 | Edit
We saw Mr. Badger at the library today. He's tall with ginger hair and glasses. He runs the Broadland chess club.
I called over; "Hey, so, how's the old Brock doing?"
Heather scowled at me.
"You shouldn't let him hear you call him that. He might be offended. We only refer to him as 'Brock' behind his back!"
*I wonder if he likes broccoli?

Nancy Pelosi loves the Donald…

By SARIN | Published: FEBRUARY 5, 2020 | Edit
Sat behind him during the State of the Union address looking as if she could spit.
Tore his speech to shreds as an act of defiance.
Bitter and twisted at the lack of success.
Only small hands, but that's a lot of pussy!

You won't play the other David (May) because he was at our club tonight, where I soundly beat off my opponent with a great win, cornering his king with my two rooks on the same file.

David Owen told me not to give away my pieces before we started, but that's just what I did, sacrificing my bishop to bring his king out into the open!

I hate these problems with the Internet.

Just going for supper. Oh, my game against David Payne isn't looking as good as I thought. We are level in pieces though.

My days are like that!
any news?

Was so cold on my bike tonight. I would send you a picture from last night, but the Reeve Code of ethics maintains control of the prints.

Could I possibly keep the film a secret, just in case we ever do get the chance to watch it some time. We have a DVD here which we never use. It's an idea… Its a beautiful story with many memorable scenes. I would describe it before….just back from my victory at the club playing for our 'Gladiator' side. Its a great feeling when you win. Needless to say I was gloating all the way downstairs and into the bar. haha!
Game with David still going on. It's a real battle. I aren't out of the wood yet.
Hunting for car keys all day. Mum's idea of a joke. She changed all her bedroom furniture around again today. I have had to order some new keys. I said to her; "you're paying for them mate!"
I can't get them here till Friday. Lots of jobs I need to do. Still awaiting pictures of Santa..

Dear Mr. King,

- Thank you for sponsoring me in return for some nice treats.

Lammergeyer Man

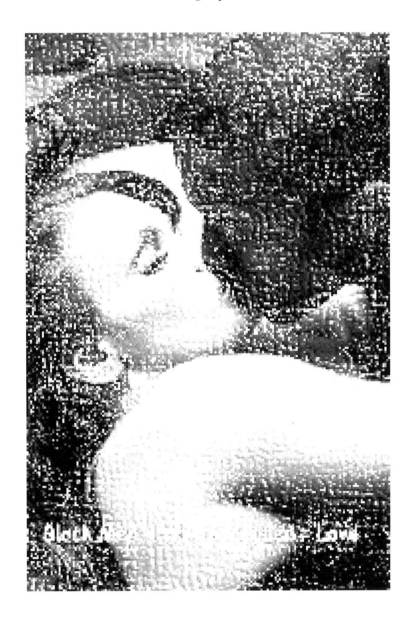

JUST PRIOR TO MY GREAT VICTORY AGAINST KILLER MILLS THE OTHER NIGHT. THE FELLOW AT THE BACK ON THE RIGHT HAS JUST RETURNED FROM WHITBY, WHERE APPARENTLY HIS BOAT LANDED A FEW DAYS BEFORE.

GARY GLITTER

Took a girl's virginity at 14 and ran off with it.

"THAT'S A BIT OLD FOR LOSING ONE'S VIRGINITY, ISN'T IT?"

IDLIB BRIDES

SCAT IN THE HAT

All Western donations gratefully inserted.

CHINA CONFIDENT IT HAS THE PLAGUE

Its been a cold dark wet old day. I just try to keep things running as best I can. Had things to do with my mum. Who'd a thought I would ever turn into a bluddy mummy's boy. Me, you and Keith are all quite obsessive people. You have to be if you want to do something well. There are a lot of very different people at the Board-meeting. Some of them look as if they have escaped from somewhere. Am getting a few pains in my head while I am writing. sometimes they come on during the night as well. I'm not sure who Russell and Cosmo are. Some people beat Callum quite convincingly, but the best I've ever done is a draw, even when I had been well ahead. He thrashed poor Rupert the other night. Just a few more chores to do. My sister doesn't help. She is even refusing to read any of my e-mails. For sure, I aren't the only one to have difficulties within the family.

There must be a reason why so many people are gathered in one place

Keith began two games of Scrabble with me today at the library and both times he shot off to play with someone else.
Heather said, "that's just the way he is..."

We grieve the death...

By USULI TWELVES | Published: FEBRUARY 3, 2020 | Edit

Of young *Sudesh Amman*, shot dead yesterday while rampaging through the streets of London with a knife. What kind of life did this poor young man have to make him so desperate and bitter?

It was lovely to see you today and to play together at the Board Meeting J

You are a hero biking there and back, I knew the weather would be bad, and that you would have a nasty cold damp headwind. Nine o'clock! We were only just in Lidl by then! Bostik left here only about twenty minutes ago ...

No, I didn't watch the Pete/Bruce game but they were going through it in the bar. Bruce won, and yes, it was a graded game, Round 3 of the Swiss, same as I was playing against Callum.

Bostik and I looked through the Callum game and I was comforted a little when he would have made exactly the same rook-losing blunder that I made ...

Just had an email from Steve Moore – you will remember he came with us to Whittlesford last year. He has entered again this year, as have I, it's the weekend of the 7th-8th March. Are you going and, if so, may we please come with you?

Glad you made it safely home, first thing I did was to look for an email from your goodself and was relieved to see two of them J

I'm bloodletting tomorrow, Bostik is picking me up at 14:15. Mr Badger has ordered us all to attend and play our Club Championship games – I'm not sure I'll be in any state to do that. Bostik is playing Martin Griffin, so maybe I'll be able to watch that.

Hope you are all right, you should sleep better after such an epic expedition!

That's brilliant that you'll be going to Whittlesford again J

I'm so pleased J

Shall I tell Steve he can come with us? He was good company last year and we can pick his brains on the way!

I'm sending you the entry form herewith, just in case you don't have it! J

No, I don't mind your jokes, but I hope Mr Badger wasn't hurt by your calling him Brock out loud – usually only his enemies (of whom he has a surprising number ...) call him that, and he knows it ... Brocks are probably best not provoked! We're off shortly to Coltishall – Bostik is playing Martin Griffin in the Club Championship. I don't know whether I'll play anyone, I don't feel much like it really.

Well, today's bloodletting was a failed mission. We were made to sit in a freezing cold corridor to fill in our forms – I really think air-conditioning is totally superfluous in the middle of February. And we had to drink a pint of freezing cold water. Consequently, when I reached the needle-lady, I was so cold that all my veins had shrunk. She had a good feel around my right arm but couldn't find any likely candidates, so switched to the left. That wasn't much better but she found one that she decided to go for. But it was useless, she was digging around with the needle but nothing would come out. So I still get a credit for it, and am rebooked for a fortnight's time. That's never happened to me before – I usually have pretty good veins.

See you soon.
Love from Heather x
----- Original Message ----

116

A dangerous lack of bio-diversity

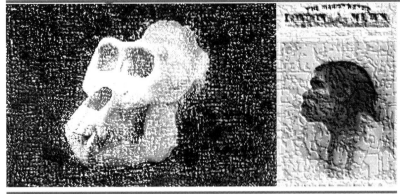

By RUMPLESTILTSKIN | *Published: FEBRUARY 2, 2020* | *Edit*

Equal rights groups are up-in-arms about the dangerous lack of diversity strutting around at the recent award ceremonies. They complained about a lack of colour, the shocking number of white people, and the disproportionately small number of untalented female directors willing to get up on stage and cry their eyes out.

Comments

Just had an e-mail from Charles, and a lovely e-card from Tona.
Took my mum out for a run to see my step-sister's new house.
I haven't had chance to get stuck into those chess magazines
and things you sent me for my birthday yet, but they were
warmly appreciated. Thankyou!
I don't know what you do on a Sunday. I imagine you getting up
at dawn and reaching for your cubes before you get out of
bed, then competing in some tournament or other by nine.
Its a cold wind out there! I have just been out on my bike to post
Tona's birthday card. Still time to do some more jobs and play a
few on-line games.
Sally looked pleased as punch at the ring Dannie bought her bought her.

Andy.

I WILL HAVE MY CAMERA TONIGHT IF YOU WANT ME TO TAKE A PHOTO OR TWO.
OTHERWISE I AM HAPPY TO USE THE ONE IN YOUR E—MAIL, BUT THERE IS SOMETHING BEHIND YOUR LEFT EAR WHICH I
WOULD RATHER NOT INCLUDE.

Jonathan.

The shape coming out of my ear is just a piece of ectoplasm. I'm happy, if you are. I hope you weren't offended by my 'running commentary remark' in the bar tonight. I should talk!!!

The so-called radicalisation of young Asian men

By USULI TWELVES | *Published: FEBRUARY 3, 2020* | *Edit*

Will you please get it through your thick heads.

It's simply a matter of having a different point of view!

Perfect in every way...

I first met Kath when I started in OT many years ago. I was lucky to get the job. I'd rung up for an application form several times. Each time she promised to send me it nothing arrived. In the end I managed to get a form from the Manager. She was always very nice to my face. She was courteous, and smiled at everyone. She had the most beautiful red hair and was loved by all the staff. Denzil showed me a letter she had sent him. It was covered in kisses. She was married with two children. Her husband was always in her thoughts, she said. Each time I left the office and closed the door behind me I could hear the howl of laughter. I wondered who it was coming from. We had to choose our best photo to go inside the staff welcome board. I only had two photos taken but was fairly satisfied with one. The other one was awful. I asked her to bin it. Kath asked me to choose which one I wanted in the board. I was very specific. I didn't want the photo where my eyes were half closed and I looked like some kind of maniac. When the board went up and everyone's photo was sealed inside, I saw to my horror that they had included the rotten photo I didn't like. My Manager (Janet Klitcher) said that someone had reported me for leaving a patient unattended in the bath, while I nipped next door for some towels.She told me that she would escort me from the building, and that if I tried to return the police would be called.

DIRTY COPS

By GODFREY WINKLEBACKER | *Published: FEBRUARY 6, 2020* | *Edit*

As yet another senior figure in politics has to step down due to an 'inappropriate' relationship, we wonder who has the right, here at BUNDERCHOOK HQ, to tell us what is *appropriate*, and *inappropriate*. Is it the morally desirable snitch, listening down the phone-line, the acceptable Catholic priest, with the choir-boy cavorting on his knee, or the sexually-explicit bent cop, visiting his bit on the side, while telling everyone else how to behave…no action taken!

Pretended to like being filmed at first. These idiots snoop into all your e-mails and personal information at will, and twist it all to suit themselves. There isn't an MP or Member of the Establishment in the country who will say a word in your defence. Taking the urine out of them is your public duty. Not only are the gang among the biggest liars on the planet they are required by law to say who they are and give their number. They often use terrorism as an excuse for bullying and intimidation.
It may feel that you are on your own sometimes, but there are lots of people who question authority, and walk around with their eyes open. Don't bother complaining on-line, because they won't bother answering. The corona-virus means they have not got time to do what they are paid for, because they are too busy tossing away at their computers.
"We only care about your welfare. How are you feeling today?"
The guy's trying to make a point. We are allowed to film the police.
If you've ever watched a pack of wolves operate. The first one comes to check out, to see if you are worth eating. Then there's another one or two hovering in the distance. Before you know it the whole mob are encircling you, waiting to have their share of the spoils.

What a load of baloney...

By ADUMLA | *Published: FEBRUARY 6, 2020* | *Edit*

Two more votes for their side, and the Democrats would have been home and dry. A word of advice Mr President. Next time you want to find any dirt on Biden, ask in person....or screw his wife.

SPYING ON A GIRL IN THE SHOWER

By <u>BIRD DUNG</u> | Published: FEBRUARY 6, 2020 | *Edit*

You can get struck off for it you know! Have your life totally ruined and destroyed.

VOYEURISM A CRIMINAL OFFENCE

FACE-BOOK POST

Well, as you can see, up again at the sound of a kettle in the kitchen. Might have to give it a miss this Saturday as I'm hoping to go out to the Unicorn on Friday, and don't know how late I'll be back. I'm going to see the group Egypt, who have two former Groundhogs in the band. Hopefully, I'll catch up with everything the following week. We do think alike. When you were talking about how you decided the best move, then your hand went and did something else sounds just like something I would say. In my game against the mighty Bruce Carman, I beat him fair and square. He was even grumbling about how I was a piece up! It was only a friendly though, the last time we played. He wasn't trying to experiment. What he did do though, after losing the game, was go back to a point in the game where he thought he made a mistake, and play it again from there. I'm not sure if Egypt are a blues band. The Fish connection could be right. Might it be Allan Fish on bass? I don't know how long they have been around.

Good to feel in charge of your life.
Bostik is slipping.

Why should you need someone's permission before mentioning their name?

By <u>BIRD DUNG</u> | Published: FEBRUARY 7, 2020 | *Edit*

The newspapers never do it. Historians don't either. People are not going to give their permission, especially if you are wanting to spill the beans.

MARTIN W. ALKER fide-master

Hi Andy and thanks for that.

Aaww, we'll all be disappointed if you can't come tomorrow – I have some good puzzles to bring and also my games vs Mr Badger and Callum Fruish. We Harriers have two matches next week, but I think I'll be playing in only one of them, and shall be Reserve in the other. Did you write down your game with Bruce? Well done beating him!

My big computer, as you know, is a vast and wondrous entity, and I managed to find my previous correspondence with Alan Fish, of Egypt. Yes, definitely Alan Fish, definitely a blues band. Alan also used to run the Norfolk Gig Guide – I don't know whether he still does. Last time we corresponded was in 2007 ...

I'm off to see Tona shortly – I bought some special "hand-finished pies" to give her a belated birthday lunch today. I expect she will try to insist on paying me for them K

They are more like a deep flan than a pie, they are in a casing of poppy-seed pastry and have a cheese and herb crumbled topping. They are lovely! I like the Sweet Potato, Feta and Sunflower Seed ones the best, but the Cauliflower Cheese and Oregano are pretty good, too.

My autonomic hand is not just something I say, it is a very real problem. I described it to Martin Walker FM, and he has, I think, found the cause. I'm sure he's right that it is a function of my nerves. I was certainly nervous on Monday against Callum, when it was at its worst. And I was very nervous the first time it happened, at a County Match ... Move 1, I picked up the c-pawn intending 1.c4 ... but as it passed over c3, the pawn slipped from my trembling fingers and landed, right way up, smack bang in the centre of c3. Obviously, now it had left my hand, I couldn't pick it up again to correct it – so 1.c3 it had to be. Both my opponent and I stared at it, dumbfounded. He probably couldn't believe that a dumb blonde could play 1.c3 in such an important game. But he was much higher graded than I was and soon got to work, demolished all my kingside and checkmated me. I looked it up when I got home, 1.c3 is called the Saragossa Attack so I suppose is respectable ... I have never played it since – but Bostik sometimes plays it against me to tease me!

Then, as I hadn't been expecting to play on Wednesday night (when Mr Badger had summoned all Club Championship contenders to play off some of their matches), I was not at all nervous – knowing I should have been bloodletting, I had intended watching Bostik and Martin Griffin's game and not playing at all. However, Mr Badger said that I still had a game to play against himself, I had Black this time. No time to get nervous, we were straight into it ... and I had no problems with disobedience from my hand, which consistently put the pieces I wanted where I wanted them.

Nay, Bostik isn't slipping ... it is I whose mighty power is overcoming his magnificent efforts ... J

Have a good day and a nice evening with your cock out.

'WHY IZ YUZ NOT BLACK LIKE AS PAPPY?'

I am a nurse

By ADUMLA | Published: FEBRUARY 11, 2020 | Edit

I am a nurse, and I work alongside the Authorities to incarcerate anyone thinking of taking their own life. Whenever you've had enough of this awful stinking world, I will help to make your life even more miserable by bringing the pigs round to section you.

Spoke to Dan the Man...

By ADUMLA | Published: FEBRUARY 11, 2020 | Edit

Crick was parked on his seat at the bar last night spying on everyone and spreading stories. I told Dan about the rumour Crick had been spreading around, that he was gay.
"Am I seeing things?" I said, rubbing my eyes. "Isn't that Crick without his mother??? I saw her combing his hair in the market place the other day."
I asked some of the lads what age they thought he was. Most of them said he looked about 55.
"And still a virgin!"

Senior ranking Cop

By ADUMLA | Published: FEBRUARY 11, 2020 | Edit

Sacked; for showing signs of normal sexual attraction towards women.
- unable to distinguish between straight and dyke
- placed his arm around a waist
- twanged a couple of bra straps
- tried to kiss a female constable

snitches

By PETER SMITH | Published: FEBRUARY 11, 2020 | Edit

I over-heard the Little Shitzah talking to Aunty on the phone tonight. I was just after I had made her supper.
"I'll keep a diary," she said, "and write down everything he does.!"

Chinese cop caught chomping on a dog

By GODFREY WINKLEBACKER | Published: FEBRUARY 8, 2020 | Edit

They've been eating them for ages in our country.

"Bullying wrong!" snaps Commander-in-Chief.
"We will arrest anyone guilty of showing aggression."

Ginger Vitus edit

NORMAL-TOWN

By USULI TWELVES | Published: MARCH 23, 2020

Here in Normal-town, people do as they are told. They never disobey the curfew. They never put other people at risk. They always think about others.

PAIN IN THE BUTT,

The Little Shitzah has made it plain to me that you are not very welcome here, especially after the terrible row you had with her the last time you were here, when you said to me that 'you were never coming back, and that 'I was on my own from now on.' I only wish you meant what you said. I am quite able to manage Mum's care without your daily interference and 'monitoring' from hundreds of miles away. We are able to get on far better on our own. You can communicate with us via e mail if you can be bothered. Simply announcing you are coming is just not appropriate at this moment. I will not run away from my own home as you suggested while you root through the house on a search for the will.

HIGH SCHOOL SNEAK by Ginger Vitus Feb 9 2020 Edit

DIDN'T YOU POST THIS ON MY WEB PAGE LILLY...

Oh, dear, what is this? I'm so upset and offended, not.

WE LIKE THIS IMAGE, HOWEVER...

'If someone deceives you, deliberately lies to you and causes you distress, you must 'forgive' them'
David Smirk, Sniggering Boy's lane, ORTHODOX CHRISTIAN STABLE, New Hampton.

THIS IMAGE CONTAINS 'FEMALE EXPLOITATION' OF THE VERY WORSE KIND. YOU WILL REMAIN IN FACE-BOOK JAIL FOR THREE DAYS.

'All the better for hearing from you. So, you are lounging about, eating chocolates and watching films with the boys all day. I bet you hardly ever see Virginija these days....ha-ha! I may be there tomorrow, but the weather is so bad. I bought a new car last week. There are so many regulations these days. Funnily enough, I came across something you had written to me earlier. It was about your time back home, when you were only small, and you went away to play in chess tournaments all over Russia. You must have been very independent and grown up for your age to stay away like you did.'

Always here for you.

What's always impressed me most about Donald...

By GODFREY WINKLEBACKER | Published: FEBRUARY 12, 2020 | Edit

Is the number of women he's supposed to have groped.

"So much culture behind African hair!"

By GODFREY WINKLEBACKER | Published: FEBRUARY 12, 2020 | Edit

You can grow it as long as you like at school now.

BLACK PUBES MATTER

BIDEN AND SON: *100YRS EXPERIENCE IN THE SALE OF ARMS.*

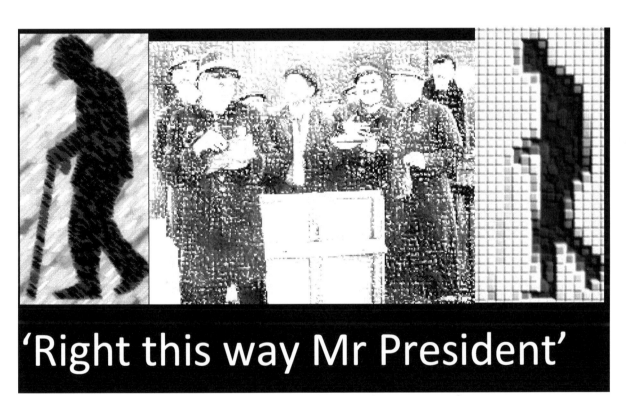

'Right this way Mr President'

Cor, rather you than me in Norwich today. The wind was bitter. How about this for an exercise?

Write a letter to:

1 Your employer, tendering your resignation on various grounds, such as sexual harassment.

2 To the council, complaining about noise in the street below, keeping you awake at night.

3 To a college, asking them about courses you are interested in and giving them a bit of background information about yourself as an escapee from domestic violence.

Make it all up if you like. The main thing is that you get things in the right place including your address and date. Letter writing can be very important. Its something we use quite a lot in everyday life. I keep bugging Ruta about a film I think you would all enjoy. We should get together some time and watch it. Very best wishes!

Andy

Yes, I am certainly looking forward to being with you on Saturday. Still a numbingly cold day outside, but at least the harsh wind has gone. I think I have met this Gerald Moore, and he's a good player.
I am somewhat similar to Callum, in that I like to wage an all out attack. I had a very interesting game against Matt Rausch the other night. He's a truly great player.
I only had one move for check-mate! All I had to do was keep my king out of trouble from his knight and bishop, which I was hoping to do, as am something of an escape artist, but he has such a sublime understanding of the squares. I did put up a good fight though.
Don't feel too bad now, but am awful in the mornings, or just after I get up. I never used to be like that. Its one of the characteristics of Parkinson's I think. Salivating, difficulty swallowing and missing out
I just told my mum you can beat anyone at chess!

Only one black actor saved the Oscars

By BIRD DUNG | Published: FEBRUARY 12, 2020 | Edit

Is that right...?

Nandi Ntoni *Look. I don't want to hold you back. I know you are a very talented black lady, with lots of strings to your bow. If I was you I would take up the offer for now.*

Dear Community Church Leaders, (February 2020)

I am writing to complain about a member of your staff: Mr. Andrew Crick, who I saw in the bar of my club on Monday night. I overheard him talking about me and spreading vicious rumours with some of the bar staff and customers. This isn't the first time he has done this. A few months ago he threatened me in the supermarket, even though I had not spoken to him. I would really appreciate if you could have a word with him before I have to take this matter any further, as his behaviour is certainly not that of an orthodox moss-backed born again bible-thumping Christian of the standard type? That goes for any other members of the church too, who want to go spreading gossip around town. **There is no need to reply and if I see him in the street again and ring my bell he will no doubt run up to the shop and threaten me again because he intercepted my letter...**

EXPOSED TO A DIFFERENT POINT OF VIEW

Winner Dave says Boris hates blacks

By PETER SMITH | Published: FEBRUARY 19, 2020 | Edit

Nothing fixed about that...

On the band wagon

By SARIN | Published: FEBRUARY 19, 2020 | Edit

Rape victims stay in touch with their attacker for career advancement...
Says Nancy Pelosi look-a-like.
EXTINCTION REBELLION: COME, AND GET NOTICED

'Oh, the cruel bitterness of this world. The times this happens to us. You can never write an opponent off. We know that, but they still bluddy mash us. She sounds a bright girl. Against you of all people. Was that the Nightingales where again? These kids have so much of an advantage growing up in homes like that. I always think May is beatable. I just haven't found a way yet. He will be just as scared of you, I would have thought. All quiet on the Western front, but a cold wind outside the door. I am looking forward to seeing that game! I hope to bring one along too!' All the best for now Heather.

The thing to understand....birth, life, death. Change is always with us. Nothing remains the same. We were just talking about Sam. If we lose him it will be a sad day for both of us. I feel fearful for Tona all on her own. It will be awful if anything happens to Honeybun. She seems such a young cat as well. I support the Government in what they are trying to do. I am going to self isolate with my mum and only go out on essential journeys.I took her over to the coast for some fresh air and bumped into Virginija. Its getting very difficult trying to explain things to my mum. These are quite serious days aren't they. at least we can always keep in touch on here. I will drop Tona a line in a minute. sending you more photos.I hope you like them.

Sweet and sour is best with mushrooms

A terrorist related incident...

"Okay, just hand over the phone, so we can snoop through all your private messages..."

Just look what we caught on the security camera at the back gate.
As I remarked the next time they lumbered round; "I think we have your best side Johnny!"

Meth fueled, mud covered, naked Florida Man shakes off two Tasers, bites K-9 and fist fights officer, then spits on another...

Oh, the useless fuk. why did he bite K-9 when he could have ripped their balls off in his mouth!
I wouldn't waste my spit.

Too ugly for words

ICE SHARD KILLS CHILD

Latest news!

Bird-girl receives honorary doctorate. This has nothing to do with her Bangladeshi heritage, or that she's young, female and from the right neck of the woods...

The snobbery of *diSadVaNtage*

BABY CURLS R BEST

Battle of Waterloo

By GODFREY WINKLEBACKER | Published: FEBRUARY 21, 2020 | *Edit*

Prior to the battle Scot's Guard, Mathew Clay, was ordered by his commanding officer to 'kill-a-pig,' so that the men could fill their bellies full of pork. A lot of the meat they ate was raw but it was better than starving to death.
Its simply just a matter of fulfilling one's honourable duty....I guess.

Hi Heather,

Just had an e mail from Sally. Dannie has a bad cough and a cold. He's just back from China but is still as leftie as ever... Its been very bitter and blustery up here. I managed to get round and do a few jobs, but bit of a headache coming on this evening. Am in the middle of a thrilling on-line game, which I would love to go through with you on Saturday. Woke with bad aching and discomfort in my chest this morning. I've had it before, but usually only when I'm very tired. I still try to exercise and lift my weights each day. I didn't mind repeating that exercise with the buttons. I think it has finally sunk in, and the one with the square. I still think I ought to do it again though, just to make sure...

I'm just trying to do the best I can. I did want to come tomorrow but might leave it for a week, and bring some games in then. I sent my money in for Whittlesford today.

February 9 2020 Andy Babychipmunk V Darkstar Turkey

1. e4 e5 2. Qh5 Nc6 3. Bc4 Qe7 4. Na3 Nf6 5. Qf3 a6 6. Nh3 d6 7. Ng5 Ng4 8. Bxf7+ Kd8 9. Bd5 Nd4 10. Nf7+ Ke8 11. Qh3 Nxf2 12. Qh5 Nxh1 13. Nxh8+ Kd8 14. Kd7 15. Qg4+ Ke8 16. Qh5 Kd7 17. Nc4 Nxc2+ 18. Kd1 Nxa1 19. Qf5+ Ke8 20. Ncxd6+ cxd6 21. Nxd6+ Qxd6 22. Qf7+ Kd8 23. b3 Qe7 24. Qh5 g6 25. Qf3 Qc7 26. Qxf8+ Kd7 27. Qf7+ Kd6 28. Ba3+ Qc5 29. Bxc5+ Kxc5 30. Qxh7 Nf2+ 31. Kc1 Nd3+ 32. Kd1 Kd4 33. Qxg6 Bd7 34. Qb6+ Nc5 35. d3 Rf8 36. Qb4+ Kxd3 37. Qxc5 Rf1#

>dandjatsarin7642.com

By <u>BIRD DUNG</u> | *Published: FEBRUARY 23, 2020* | <u>*Edit*</u>

Well, Mr. David Doctor Strange-love,

Your cover is well and truly blown.
That night you came to sit next to me when I first met up with Heather was a dead give away. The pigs have contacts all over. It was nice of you to buy me a drink though, but did you have to sit so close all night long…Great to hear about your early career, before you took to smashing down people's doors with a sledge-hammer. I did offer to help you with your shopping after your recent fall. It was hard for me not to like you. I've often found that with the filth. Time I woke up.

DEAR LOCAL CONSTABULARY…

By <u>ADUMLA</u> | *Published: FEBRUARY 24, 2020* | <u>*Edit*</u>

Dear local Sow-trough,

I have written to the council several times about some of the young people on the estate who seem to be getting out of hand. Only today I saw one of them sneak past wearing a T-shirt with the slogan:

'Pigs are shit,' and 'Oik' emblazoned in big letters across his back.

Before you know it this could lead to complete anarchy and the breaking down of all the natural moral codes which govern society. Isn't this a 'hate' crime?

Last week I observed another juvenile delinquent sporting one which said:

'Pigs are scum,'…err, humiliatingly obvious I know. What are you going to do about it?

Yours Sincerely,

Marion Carston Smudge-winkle

Church Warden

Bull-dozer used to clear away debris

By <ins>USULI TWELVES</ins> | Published: FEBRUARY 24, 2020 | <ins>Edit</ins>

I was out on the West-bank today, emptying the rubbish and taking the higher moral ground. I saw some men in uniform having a bit of fun shunting a sack of offal around on the floor. They were laughing their heads off...as it got caught under the wheels.

The problem with poorer families

By <ins>SARIN</ins> | Published: FEBRUARY 24, 2020 | <ins>Edit</ins>

Mum always insisted we use the same bath-water, starting with the youngest. I never knew whether I was sharing the slime with some of my sister's boyfriends spermatozoa.

Hi Andy

Aaww, watching sport all night is not going to do you any good ☹
Did you watch the boxing? Good result for Mr Fury ay ☺

Yes, a very nasty wind. I did get out in the garden for an hour or so this afternoon, trimmed a shrub or two so that I can now walk down the garden path, planted out some hyacinths and aquilegias in the front garden from a pot, pulled out some weeds, inspected the barns but so far the toxic noxious creeper looks fairly dormant.

Probably be a good thing if you can get a quiet day tomorrow. Ah, I have bloodletting in the afternoon, which will NOT be good preparation for my Match in the evening. I am on Board 1, Black, and am likely to face any of these three opponents:
Jacob Davison   87F J
Matthew Haines   86D
Costakis Stephanides   82E

Can't remember the last time I had White – not that I particularly want White, I'm quite happy with Black. But my last nine standard-play games have resulted in seven losses and two draws ☺

I think tomorrow is going to be a tough day for me! I'll probably give the GlassHouse a miss. Maybe my new Cubes will come ... maybe.

Just been having a little play on the laptop, first time for over a week. I like it but just don't have the time. But back on this big one for the real stuff! i.e. writing to you ☺
Off to bed now – you, and me.

PS Sally's new ICF grade is -20. Far too high for a pee-wee, in my opinion.
Sorry to say there won't be space for you at our wedding reception.

Love from Heather x

Great day for 'justice'

By RUMPLESTILTSKIN | Published: FEBRUARY 24, 2020 | Edit

Harvey found guilty of third-degree rape...(touching the genitals without consent, looking the wrong way, arguing).
I challenge anyone to disagree.
- Women never lie or exaggerate
- It's wrong to seek your own selfish sexual gratification
- You will always have the media on your side
- Ticket tout sent down for making a profit

Congratulations. You can now be labelled as a rapist for life!

Singing her new song; "I've had it done to me too!"

Hi Andy!

I AM STILL ALIVE. SO MANY THINGS HAPPENED DURING THESE TWO WEEKS. MY BROTHER WENT ON HOLIDAY AND LETT TWO DOGS FOR ME TO LOOK AFTER . ONE OF THEM IS A PUPPY. I HAD LOTS OF FUN, CLEANING, TAKING FOR A WALK AND TIDYING WHAT MESS SHE DID. HER NAME IS DAISY AND SHE IS CUTE BUT A CHEEKY YOUNG DOG , 5 MONTHS. VALIUS LEFT HER ON HER OWN FOR 10 MINUTES AND SHE STARTED TO MAKE MESS. SHE DRAGGED THE DISCS FROM TV CUPBOARD,

FOUND SOME TISSUES AND OF COURSE, SHE HAD TO TEAR SOME TO SMALL PIECES. VALIUS WAS
MAD. ANYWAY, EVENTUALLY MY BROTHER SOLD HER AND NOW SHE LIVES WITH A GOOD FAMILY.
AND OTHER DOG ROXY WAS INJURED IN CAR ACCIDENT AND HAD AN INJURY ON HER LEG. SO I HAD
TO LOOK AFTER HER LEG AS WELL. AND SHE DIOES NOT LIKE ANY PLASTER ON HER LEG AND SHE
JUST LICKS HER WOUND.
IT WAS A WAR, SO WE HAD TO TAKE SOME MEASURES AND HAD TO PUT A COLLAR ON THE NECK
TO STOP HER LICKING IT.
BUT ROXY IS A GOOD GIRL, MY CHILDREN HAD VARIOUS CUBS ON HALF TERM AND ALL OF THEM
WERE IN NORWICH. ROKAS HAD FOOTBALL FOR TWO DAYS AND ERIKAS WENT TO DETECTIVE
ACADEMY.
ERIKAS CAUGHT A SICKNESS BUG ON WEDNESDAY AND ROKAS ON FRIDAY. SO AS YOU SEE, WE
ARE NEVER BORED.
HOW IS LIFE TREATING YOU? WHAT DO YOU MEAN GOSSIP. WHAT ARE YOU TRYING TO HIDE ANDY?
I STILL DREAM ABOUT YOU EVERY NIGHT.
Ruta

'We hope to see you next week as we miss you when
you don't come. I think its less windy today , but
I don't think we can grumble when you consider what the
folks are suffering from in some parts of the country.
I looked round my flat and considered what I would miss
most should we have floods here and discovered what I
would miss would be my books. Strange as I have read
them anyway, but they are favourite ones.'

Love Tona

Show original message

("You don't know me...and you'll never know me...")

This is a picture of my friend Amber before they carted her off. It was the fumes from her house-mate's arse-hole which
finally drove her over the edge. He hasn't spoken to her in over a week now...

"The vaccine never did me any arm!"

Am thinking of asking the pigs to frame it.

133

I did mention to Steve in response to his e mail about the bye. I don't think he will mind because his friend Abdul will be there anyway..? Its a pity about your club form. Bear in mind, that anyone can give you a game, and there are so many very clever people out there. I can take a hit from anyone 800 or above on Chess.com. Especially if I give away a stale-mate with seven queens. Some brilliant players. I go through phases. I did lose a few silly games, sometimes through lack of concentration and moving too fast, but sometimes they are just too good, although they might not get me a second time. The long match I am having in which I lost my queen early on is still continuing, but he doesn't seem to want to play, now I am getting the upper hand. I haven't had a response from the Organisers, but have noted my place of honour.

holding up the pack   on the bottom rung. I hope to be there Saturday. Jupiter willing...

Dear Age UK,

I'm writing on behalf of my mother Commandant Magrit-Amis who has had her car insurance with you for many years now but is growing increasingly aberrant and mad. She lost her husband, my step-dad, a little while back due to cancer, and frustration at having his belongings constantly moved from pillar to post. When I rang today they could not locate her letter and suggested the best way to contact you would be by e-mail. I rang to see if you had received her letter as she had not heard from you.

1 Could you tell us how much you have raised the insurance for the year by, after she changed her car, so we can compare it with the old figure. It seems to have gone up by a huge amount. She simply changed the model of the car and has not suddenly become a threat to society.

2 It said in your notes that my mum had an accident in 2015 in her old car. She has no recollection of being involved in any accident whatsoever. I don't think this should have had any effect on the total anyway.

3 She had been thinking of using someone else because of this enormous increase.

4 She wondered if reverting to 'Third party fire and theft' would bring the amount down. If it did she would like to change it to that, as nearly two thousand pounds per annum, when we only nip down to the shops occasionally is rather taking the piss.

So glad you didn't bring up my past...I have now found your letter in her sewing box.

The real Spartacus

Crassus's response to the defeat of his first army was to have four thousand of his own soldiers beaten to death for cowardice.
It's always wrong to oppose Authority...

WANKERS

Top of the Form

You couldn't catch a cold running naked in the Arctic.

Heather won today!

By PETER SMITH | Published: FEBRUARY 29, 2020 | Edit

At the chess puzzles she knows so well. I liked the way her and Charles giggled, every time she did so.

I hope you're soon feeling better and able to come on Saturday. Sally and Dannie have a load of chess books to lend out, so if you want to borrow any, just say. All these are in proper notation, but they also have some in the old gobbledegook:

Learn to play winning chess - Saunders
The Official laws...various
Teach yourself chess - Hartston
Chess Jugglet - Magner
Chess Openings for Dummies -Eade
Chess for Dummies - Eade
The right way to play chess - Pritchard (updated)

Corona virus: I've always practised social distancing.

Assange protected from corona-virus

By USULI TWELVES | Published: MARCH 2, 2020 | Edit

First he was young, then he was old.
Then he was a rapist, then he was not.
We can change the law when ever we like, because we are the justice system.

Steven Kirk Scotland (1027) V Baby-Chipmunk (857)

Feb 2020

1. d4 Nc6 2. c3 d5 3. e3 Nf6 4. f3 Bf5 5. Nd2 e6 6. g4 Bg6 7. h4 h5 8. g5 Qe7 9. gxf6 Qxf6 10. Bb5 0-0-0 11. Bxc6 e5 12. Bxb7+ Kxb7 13. Qe2 exd4 14. cxd4 Bd6 15. Qb5+ Kc8 16. Qxd5 Bg3+ 17. Kd1 Rxd5 18. Ne2 Bf2 19. e4 Rb5 20. b3 c5 21. Bb2 Rd8 22. Rc1 Be3 23. Ba3 Kb7 24. Bxc5 Bxd2 25. Kxd2 Qxf3 26. Nc3 Qf4+ 27. Kc2 Qf2+ 28. Kb1 Ra5 29.   Rxc5 30. Na4 Bxe4+ 31. Ka1 Rcxd5 32. Nc5+ Kb6 33. Nxe4 Ra5 34. Nxf2 Rd2 35. a4 Re5 36. Rhe1 Rf5 37. Ne4 Rd3 38. Ka2 Rff3 39. Rb1 f5 40. Ng5 Rf2+ 41. Rb2 Rf4 42. Ka3 a5 43. Re6+ Kc5 44. Rc2+ Kd5 45. Rc8 Rd2 46. Rd8+ Kc5 47. Rxd2 Rxh4 48. Re5+ Kc6 49. Rxf5 g6 50. Rxa5 Rh1 51. Ra6+ Kc5 52. Rxg6

HARVEY WALL-BANGER

"Football!"

Lydia said....

By PETER SMITH | Published: FEBRUARY 29, 2020 | Edit

"You're a very sad little man!"
I said;
"At least I never got in a car full of Parkies, drove my partner insane, and covered the walls with red."

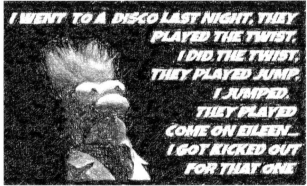

CHARITY WORKER

The books in the window are mine...

Several years ago...confessions of a Stalker

By SARIN | Published: FEBRUARY 29, 2020 | Edit

Several years ago I employed a Private Investigator to track down my ex. She went to the door with a friend carrying a briefcase, inside which lay a hidden camera. It made very uncomfortable viewing, seeing the old house, the kids, and hearing the sound of everyone. She looked harder and older than before. I had to laugh when they asked her:

"Does Gillian Taylforth live here?"

My ex partner answered; "We've lived here for eight years, but you could try down the road..."

BIG EARS *By SARIN | Published: FEBRUARY 29, 2020 | Edit*

Pete asked about the game, and said that "it was only a flash-in-the-pan..."
I said I couldn't make it, because I had a lot on next week.

Comments

Thank you Andy for your prompt action. The print seems very small; I hope I can read it.What are you worry-gutting about not being able to beat Heather at her pet end games. Of course you can't; she's studied these end games for some years and very often wins a club game as a result. Struggle to win, as I do, when playing a game but know her forte, 'The End Game'. Then if you still can't win that's because she's better than you so you (we) must try to avoid her swapping everything off which brings on the end game. We are very fortunate to have her; in fact, it's a great little group much enhanced by your presence, Andy. Next time, instead of following one of your games lets follow one or two of Heathers and discuss where she could have done better.Thanks for the corpses. There's no hurry for the return of that Speccy now. Happy days. **Charles Smutty**

Not worried. My ex's son played me on a motor-racing game he'd been playing on his X-box for months, and when I lost he was gloating, as if he'd won something, yet he'd never even been able to drive a real car...I'm not too bad at the end game. I wanted to know what I was doing wrong against her, but was just unable to understand her strategy.

JUST SO YOU KNOW

Yahoo/Sent

I keep seeing you around town Colin, don't I. How long ago is it now, that you turned up to my Writer's group and wrote about 'the Bully.'

In case you've heard a few mistruths from people down at the church, who in my opinion, are some of the worse schismatic heretics in town.

I'm not sure if you read my article in the EDP a while back, but what had I got to lose. I was so sick of people telling lies about me and so on.

I was sat there with Christine one Christmas, and all she talked about the whole time was her horrible son, Brian. I told her that if she didn't stop, I was going to go back home.

She said: "Go on then. I know you don't love me really." Which was probably right. I decided then that I was going to try and find someone else, but that's not so easy is it.

I'm aware you know her from when we used to get together, and from church.

I'd done a book-signing day, but found her conversation extremely frustrating. I don't think she's read a book in her life. I took her up to see her son. The neighbours had been making false complaints about us again, none of which were true. Her son accused me of always getting his mum into trouble. Him and his fat slob of a girlfriend have had the police up on each other more times than I've had hot dinners. He told me that I had to stop seeing his mother. He became very threatening and aggressive, so I got up and walked out, waiting for Christine outside. She never came out. The next time I went down Brenda had all my things packed up in a bag. She said it was over. I never actually spoke to Christine, nor she to me. I did visit the church, but her and Brenda ran over to report me to Jack, like two stupid little muppets. He encouraged them both. What a little creep he is.

After a few weeks I saw Christine in Tesco's. She looked very odd. I went up and said; "After seven years, in which we were in each other's company every day, you couldn't even speak to me, but you could to them..?"

When I returned the police were waiting for me at my home. They accused me of harassing her, and said that I had only known her for a few days, and that she had never been more than just a friend. They said that if I ever tried to contact her again, or to speak to her in any way they would put me in prison.

While I was with Christine down at the Bure Valley Zoo I was aware of a youngish chap parking his car outside her kitchen window. I didn't think it would be long until she spotted him. Whenever there was a man outside she would always rush to the window. She had a reputation all around town it was said. She even went with her sister's husband behind her sister's back, but told me not to tell anyone.

Well Colin. I am well shut of it don't you think.

I don't know if you saw me in the paper after competing in a National chess tournament. I took it up recently.

Am doing a good job of looking after my mum even though its very difficult at times.

Life has never been so good, although I haven't been very well the last few years.

Andy
(You'd have to own at least the remains of a skeletal structure down your back to reply though...)

＊ Hi Leo! Just had a truly bizarre notion. Dreamt you were over here in Norfolk to promote your new masterpiece.
We decided to drive to Oxford and visit Pam and Howard. When they came to the door, we said that you had just killed Rosemary Clooney, and were on the run from the Cops. I imagined seeing Howard walking straight to his phone.

Living in permanent fear

By <u>RUMPLESTILTSKIN</u> | Published: MARCH 6, 2020 | <u>Edit</u>

We were sitting round the table at the chess group, with Heather opposite me, when Charles said;

"You'd better be careful, Andy. Its a leap year, and women can ask a man to marry them…"

Comments

New Virus attacks the Italian main-land

By BIRD DUNG | Published: MARCH 6, 2020 | Edit

PUT THE BLAME ON YOU

WELCOME TO THE FIELD OF DREAMS

 **Amen!**

It's a lot harder to torture people nowadays since everyone actually enjoys being tied up and gagged.

Dear election centre. I hope you received my fifty ballot papers in plenty of time' Fred Flintstone, Georgia. U.S.A.
Trump may have increased his vote by several million, but why should that matter…

Victim of our success

Three cheers for the Gypsy King

By BIRD DUNG | Published: MARCH 1, 2020 | Edit

"Uncomfortable"
"Inexcusable!"
"A very sorry role-model"
"Not wicked enough to become a 'non-person'"
"Winner by a knock-out"
"Refused to admit his guilt"
"Spent most of his time celebrating..."

Not enuff blacks learning to swim

By GODFREY WINKLEBACKER | Published: MARCH 2, 2020 | Edit

Due to possible hydrophobia.
Push backs illegal say Christian converts.

When rape is only sexual assault

By <u>USULI TWELVES</u> | *Published: MARCH 2, 2020* | <u>*Edit*</u>

We'd been childhood sweethearts for eight years until we got married. It was only in our fiftieth year that things began to get sour. The first argument we had was about how many lumps of sugar to put in your coffee. I looked back at her behaviour on the park bench, where we courted so long ago.

- She grabbed my chest
- She groped my loin
- She slapped my ass
- She forced my cock into her gob
- She made my hands do things they were unsure about

Had a weird dream this morning that I was looking at an e mail pertaining to come from you. This is probably just an illusion caused by lack of sleep...

In case I am wrong, and I have accidentally lost it here is one from me.

I hope you are happy and nice and warm and cosy.

I am just doing the best I can over here, looking after everything.

Best wishes to you and all the family,

Love from Andy

Black and blue

When Dan came back,
Along the lane,
With steps of cheer and flurry,
The man was waiting at the end,
To ask why he'd been missing.

His books were gone,
His shoes were wrong,
That day in far old Newry.
He beat him all the way to mam,
"You're not my Dadaí Johnny."

143

: s-u-g-a-r c-o-a-t-e-d t-e-f-l-o-n

<u>rules for making a pass</u>

think before you act

never act in haste

always have an alibi

stop when you've had enough

look before you leap

hit the ball in the right direction

never pass to strangers

I thought he had a lot more skill as a boxer than people gave him credit for.

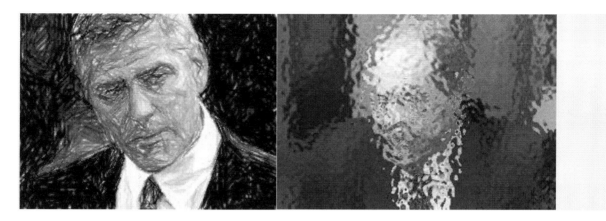

BEFORE AND AFTER

Act Centre due to close

By <u>GODFREY WINKLEBACKER</u> | Published: MARCH 11, 2020 | <u>Edit</u>

Not because of Corona virus, but due to 'staffing-issues,' after your recent comment was finked.

Porn isn't degrading to women...they get paid much more for filming than men.

...its degrading to men because it targets men with higher and unfulfilled sex drives!

I don't know. I've always seen it as a back-handed compliment being asked to take part in a porn film. Also, porn targets everyone. Women watch as much porn as men.

Hide or report this

'People shouldn't die!'

OUT TRUMPED

MINI-MIKE: "WE MEASURE FROM THE NECK UP"

nice to think "I've got half a billion dollars to set on fire in some short meaningless way... what should I do?"

Dear Mr May,

We are currently holding auditions for a new series of 'the Adam's family,' and wish to know if you would like to be considered for any of the roles?

TOO DISGUSTED FOR WORDS

'Had a great time at the Whittlesford tournament; it was so nice last year I agreed to go back. Offered Heather a draw in the last round, and she almost snapped my hand off. I was ahead, and gaining ground, but I just thought how nice it would be for us both to go home happy. I had a check-mate against May, who you played. All I had to do was take his Queen. He told me he would have resigned on the spot, but I fluffed it, having had him under the cosh from the start. It would have been mate with only two minutes gone on my clock. He won at Golder's Green. You should have seen his face. I will not forget that. I thought he had ants in his trousers. I gave him the thumbs down sign. Having missed a check-mate which I should have seen, I then had another chance later to finish him off, and instead, gave him my queen for nothing. I am really too highly strung. Should have been put down years ago. I get really excited and can't control, don't want to control my emotions.

Richard Freeman came out of the hall to ask me if I was an Actor.
He said they could even hear my voice on the other side of the Pennines.'

Lightning strike

Hi Steve!

I hope you had a good contest.

I had a check-mate, or so I thought, against Ed Knox (who turned out to be
a really pleasant fellow) with his king on the back row,
lifted up my Queen prematurely and lobbed it into position, thus
telegraphing what I was going to do.
Then I gave it away the next go. I was so exasperated with my stupidity I
resigned on the spot. I wanted to have a really good rant in the contest
room, but of course you are not allowed, although I did see you pale
somewhat looking in my direction..!
I was winning against Heather, but offered her a draw; she almost snapped
my hand off....I thought it would just be nice for us both to go home
happy. We had a great weekend.

All the best,

Andy+

The amount of gossiping done at the Act Centre
By ADUMLA | Published: MARCH 10, 2020 | Edit

That's what happens when you put so many women all in one place.

The Society of Friends
By SARIN | Published: MARCH 9, 2020 | Edit

We'll always help....to label you, especially if you've been in any trouble!

The door left open
By SARIN | Published: MARCH 9, 2020 | Edit

When I came back the Little Shitzah said Janet round the corner had left all the
lights on in her house today.

'How did you know that?' I asked.

The war in Syria...

By RUMPLESTILTSKIN | Published: MARCH 17, 2020 | Edit

Has been cancelled, due to COVID-19!

 **Love at first bite**

HEROIN

Taken with pleasure

NO 90YR OLD AGEING SAGGING DEMENTIA SUFFERER SHALL DIE, EVEN IF IT MEANS THE LOSS OF EVERY JOB AND GULAG IN THE COUNTRY. EVERY HUMAN LIFE IS PRECIOUS TO A CARING AND MAGNIFICENT HOMINID.

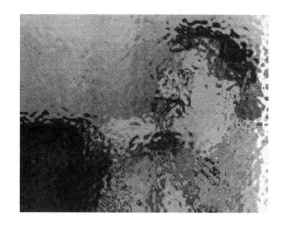

Let's have a few billion more to hack down the trees.

Bunderchook Starword Poet Amazon UK

Time for your six-monthly diabetes review

woman cut off mother's head and took it to allotment...

New virus mutates down the Inter-net

By BIRD DUNG | Published: MARCH 11, 2020 | Edit

Can now be caught through e-mails, text messages and sneezing on your computer.

Nadine Rittcers ⭐ I never watched a porno but I'm so straight I think only man on man porn would be for me 😂

Snoop dogs working for the State keep arresting people for it...its considered a hate crime against women over here. still, who takes any notice of a state ruled by

schmucks

V Anna Rechel (60e, daughter of IM Bernd Rechel 246e!)

I wonder if the Corona-virus will affect the chess matches.

When I saw David Love in town yesterday, he said the Aylsham team lost 4-0. I said he was a good player. he took Callum apart! so many good players.
was okay till heard mum on phone to my sister. she is so two faced.
Am feeling better today after a good deep sleep.

Meeting up with my Spiritualist friend Roger tomorrow. am doing some more work on his horoscope. I hope you are having a great evening. Just on my way to check on the Yorkshire puds.....for now.

Hi Hayley,

Sorry to hear there will be no lunch or activities this week due to....'staffing problems...'
I hope it's something which can be remedied quickly and no injuries have been sustained.
See you next time. ☺

Best Wishes,

ANDY VON BUNDERCHOOK

Trump can swat away petty viruses with a waft of his hair lacquer. look at the way he dealt with Clinton and Pelosi.

Sky news: Trump no good!

By SARIN | Published: MARCH 13, 2020 | Edit
1. The American economy will fail
2. Test for Corona-virus a waste of time
3. We don't like him
4. New Chinese super-bug tested first on peasants
5. Stoked up trouble by saying we should not give in to the virus.

Kerry lost her phone with all her contacts....

By SARIN | Published: MARCH 13, 2020 | Edit
Do we believe her?

The amount of gossiping done at the Act Centre

By Expletive Deletive | Published: MARCH 10, 2020 | Edit

That's what happens when you put too many Cooks all in the same space.

ANDY CRICK
I wouldn't give you a job sweeping up johnnies in Magdalen Road car park.

MESSAGE TO AZURITE **BLACK** *'Maybe it was the junk which obscured my vision inside your tent. You sure know how to grunt. How many dogs did you say you had...I would never have guessed you were in Malta.'*

Of course 'J' snitched on me!

By GODFREY WINKLEBACKER | Published: MARCH 16, 2020 | Edit

Where else did he get the idea of running a library group.

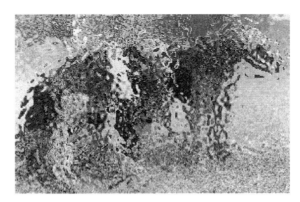

"I wonder if we'll get any statutory sick pay?"

Lack of transparency

By GODFREY WINKLEBACKER | *Published: MARCH 16, 2020* | *Edit*

Talking to the Little Shitzah, and Pain-in-the-butt, is like dealing with two moonstruck cowboys, yet it is they who are in charge of running the asylum.
I asked the Shitzah if she had read the letter from the Vet, which advised removing Sam's eye. She said she had changed her mind…?
I told her that she was in a vulnerable group, and that the Government were instructing us to 'self-isolate.' She laughed and said.."bring it on!" After that she pulled the plug out. **Comments**

Spoke to Roger

By GODFREY WINKLEBACKER | *Published: MARCH 16, 2020* | *Edit*

Saw the mighty Roger striding along the High Street today. All his groups abroad have been cancelled. I am still working on his horoscope for the big day. I told him about the dream I had just before coming into town. I had been sat at a table with a lady friend, who was trying to draw someone who was on the other side. I saw a girl appear, as clear as day. She hid behind a tree, over to my right, and then came out and stood before me. For a change, I wasn't afraid. A line of young people passed by on my left. She stood before me again.
I heard the sound of someone singing, I think it was *Lana del Ray;*
"I could be our China doll…"

DEMOCRATS…

By USULI TWELVES | *Published: MARCH 17, 2020* | *Edit*
Have been paying for dirt on Trump, for years.

'I had been thinking about you. If I hadn't heard from you tonight, I was still going to write. You have been so quiet recently. Have you been hiding? No! You have been snowed under with family matters. I really feel for you. It is worth bearing in mind that there is normally a lot of flu around at this period anyway. You should all get well and may not have anything too serious I hope.

Please send my regards to Valius. I hope he gets better soon. Its a bad time for restaurants.

Tyrozettes from the chemist are excellent for any mouth sores. Hot lemon and honey too. Keep drinking hot drinks! It's not easy, especially for you, but self isolating yourselves for a time may be the only answer. I notice that they are even wearing gloves in the supermarket now.

I pray that everything will improve and by summer most of it will be over.

If you can't get out I could always drop something off for you.'

Love and blessings to you and all the family

'I only come to see the Little Shitzah. You can go off somewhere while I am there. Make sure the kettle is clean. When you are gone I will drive into Norwich and buy myself ten fur coats to wear at work...mum is a little cunt'

Pain-in-the-butt *January 2020*

'Genny is an awful woman. I cannot stand her being here. With a bit of luck she will never bother us again'

THE LittLE 2-FaCED SHitzaH *March 2020*

GREAT NEWS! The British economy will slump.

Chinese labourer found to have slept with Peking duck
By BIRD DUNG | Published: MARCH 18, 2020 | Edit
Ah! Now we know where it's all been coming from.

Hi Roger!

I've had a look at your horoscope for the day in question. I've used your natal and progressed charts, with aspects made to each by transiting planets. It's a load of crap, but I'm sure you will appreciate all the work that's gone into it.

Behind the scenes is a strong desire by you to be helpful and fair, even though you may feel a sense of helplessness yourself, to some degree, caused by the bitches and bastards in our society. You really want to get along with everyone and to do the right thing, whatever that is. You have a willingness to be truthful and to listen to what is being said, although you will probably do what most people do, and ignore what you do not like. You feel a loss of power and that matters have been taken out of your hands without any control, or knowing what to expect, from the haughty public-school toff sat playing with his knob under the bench. You have a feeling of having to hold back and watch your P's and Q's, even though you need to stand up for yourself and put your side of the argument. There's a tendency to want to rush to speak and get your words in quickly before the others do, especially when you feel you are being criticized unnecessarily. You are quite rightly, very sensitive to criticism, with the possibility of over-reacting. If there's anything they don't like to hear, it's the truth.

Changes are likely to be made to the way you have fun, and spend time playing with children, but you are able put your ideas forcefully forward and think up new ways around any old problems. Of course, the Court will have the final word, and sacrifices will have to be made. You may not be entirely happy with the decision, but if you don't there isn't a darn thing you can do to about it.

You could be a bit touchy about the way things broke down in your relationship. There are sensitive issues around the home and the way things are done there. Nevertheless, you are ready to move on and start again. You recognise that this is an end to the past. You have a strong sense that what is yours should be yours and a stubbornness to resist any oppressive measures.

The settlement reached will take into account your home circumstances before reaching a final conclusion. People are trying to help you in unusual ways, and they are desperate to find you a path along which you can travel, so you can enjoy your time with your daughter. It may involve having to put yourself out and some awkwardness in certain situations, especially if your former partner decides not to turn up again, and remains laughing at you, standing in the rain, from the café on the other side of the street.

You are sensitive to the needs of others and willing to give way for their sake, but not without a fight, and some dispute. They will probably shit all over you, but then, that is the wonderful human race, we are all so proud of. You will learn to live with any changes or conditions which limit your freedom because if you don't, you will wish you had.

The desire for stability and structure, taking responsibility for loved ones, will lead to a beneficial and benign outcome. You recognise the need to protect the weak and vulnerable and it is in your heart to do so. You remain very protective towards the ones you love. The details drawn up will suit your desire to spend time with those you love, to be fun-loving, to be the bearer of creative activities and pleasures.

On the day of your appearance in Court you will have a lot of energy and the capacity to stand your ground, and speak up for yourself. Some of this energy is being fed to you from energies on the other side. This will be very helpful to you and give you added power. You will need to go there knowing exactly what you want in fine detail. Writing things down may help, as would references from people who know you well. It will be a good day for communicating your thoughts. You will speak in new and dynamic ways but will need to involve yourself sympathetically in any discussions. You will need to study any documentation thoroughly lest you are tricked.

You may have to talk about your home and the places you go to so that people can feel secure about any decision. So, it was your spirit guides who told you all about me…

By stressing the protective nature of your character, the safe refuge you can offer, you should make some head-way, in getting your feelings across. It will be helped by your generous and kind disposition, and your ability to reach a compromise. You are able to use your innate ability to see the argument from both sides, even though that is not so easy sometimes, and to seek a sensible solution for all concerned. I think you will come up with the perfect compromise!

With your Sun still trine Jupiter, it should overall, be a successful day. Good luck can be found in quiet thoughtful reflection, communicated to your listeners in peaceful and sympathetic ways. You will do what is necessary for the good of your daughter. There may be some financial gain or unexpected good luck but you need to have patience, and try to remain calm. Be careful not to get too angry or show any signs of aggression by throwing your coat over the barrier or by casting aspersions as to the sexual orientation of the bench, no matter how much you are provoked by your ex-partner sniggering at you with her family of freaks on the other side of the court-room. Try to keep a cool head. Choose your words very carefully. You might feel a bit hard done by, but you should feel reasonably confident about what's down the line.

You don't like having to be there, but its essential for you to get a fair and benign agreement so you can carry on with the rest of your life. Have a glimpse at what has gone by, as it will inform the future.

CRUNKLE BOUNDERCHUCK March 2020

BISHOP OF LONDON

By BIRD DUNG | Published: APRIL 10, 2020 | Edit
"Its okay not to be okay…" We sent our ballot papers in last Tuesday.

THE ROMAN SIEGE OF JERUSALEM

The Siege of Jerusalem in the year 70 CE was the decisive event of the First Jewish–Roman War, in which the Roman army captured the city of Jerusalem and destroyed both the city and its Temple. The Roman army, led by the future Emperor Titus, besieged and conquered the city of Jerusalem, which had been controlled by Judean rebel factions since 66.

The siege of the city began on 14 April 70 CE, three days before the beginning of Passover that year.[3][4] The siege lasted for about four months; it ended in August 70 CE on Tisha B'Av with the burning and destruction of the Second Temple.[5] The Romans then entered and sacked the Lower City. The Arch of Titus (a truly awe-inspiring sight), celebrating the Roman sack of Jerusalem and the Temple, still stands in Rome. Over one million inhabitants died in the assaults according to some estimates, and many more were forced into slavery. The leader of the Jewish force, Simon bar Giora, was ritually strangled before the Emperor. Trumpets were sounded and a great cheering was heard, from nobles and rabble alike...

Susan O'Reilly, Face-book…

I don't mind playing you on subjects such as TV soaps, beauty, fashion and celebrities, even though I prefer deeper more thought provoking areas.

The Crick followed me into the supermarket yesterday after he heard me ring my bell on my bike. He must have raced up the hill and sneaked in the back wall to get there when I did. He said that he did not appreciate what I had done and that he would tell Simon Gallagher if I touched the back of my neck again. I faced up to him and swelled up my chest without speaking. The little toad soon crept out of sight.

" I WONDER IF WE COULD SLIP a BIT In WInE-stain's DRINK?"

Pain in the arse…

By PETER SMITH | Published: MARCH 20, 2020 | Edit

'Please let us know when you expect to be here so we can book a holiday'

Budgen's Post Office staff…

By SARIN | Published: MARCH 20, 2020 | Edit

Don't seem to have a clue what they are doing. I asked several times for some information, but the lady did everything she could to avoid answering me…

OAFS

By ADUMLA | Published: MARCH 20, 2020 | Edit

You can only die when we tell you. Look, get inside, or we will beat your head to pulp.

Libby at the Post Office

By ADUMLA | Published: MARCH 20, 2020 | Edit

Why are the fittest women also the biggest bitches?

Ryan and Crick Funeral Directors Inc.

By SARIN | Published: MARCH 21, 2020 | Edit

I heard from Ryan at the town hall that the first case of corona-virus has been found at the Bure Valley Zoo. Apparently his aunty told him. Crick has been broadcasting it all round town in between having his hair parted by his mother.

False entries of the Bure Valley arse-wipes...

Dear ex-con,

We have been making entries about you since you arrived and every one of them has confirmed what was already said about you. We will have no alternative but to end your tenancy forthwith and collect our reward from the

APPROPRIATE AUTHORITIES.

FurtHer diSSeNt

1.	g6 2. e3 NF6 3. NF3 Bg7 4. Ng5 0-
0 5. Bd3 c5 6. c3 d6 7. Qb3 Nc6 8. Bc4 d5 9. Bb5 a6 10. BXc6 bXc6 11. dXc5 Bd7 12. Nd2 BF5 13. F3
Bd3 14. c4 dXc4 15. NXc4 Qd5 16. e4 BXc4 17. eXd5 BXb3 18. aXb3 cXd5 19. Bd2 e5 20. Ra4 Nd7 2
1. b4 H6 22. NH3 e4 23. Bc3 Ne5 24. BXe5 BXe5 25. b3 Bc3+ 26. Kd1 F5 27. NF4 Kg7 28. Ne6+ KF7
29. NXF8 KXF8 30. b5 a5 31. H4 e3 32. Ke2 Bd4 33. RXd4 Rd8 34. Ra1

First game against **Bath Bishops**, for **Norfolk Knights**. I presume *Organic-Hippo* resigned, because the game has closed and he is offering me a re-match.

70% OF PEOPLE WILL ALREADY HAVE IMMUNITY TOWARDS THE VIRUS. NO OVER-REACTION HERE THEN!

PrİNce CHarLeS teSted pOSİtİve bUt İS doİNg WeLL. THat WaS NearLy tHe SUcceSSİoN probLeM SOrted oUt...!

The honourable Sir Alex Salmond

By GODFREY WINKLEBACKER *|* *Published: MARCH 26, 2020* *|* *Edit*
Went through agony for two years of his life
Suffered insults and spitting on his pizza
Destroyed his family and professional reputation
Accused of numerous sexual assaults
Had to listen to a pack of lies and gross exaggeration
Political opponents laughing their cocks off
Offered bribes to give evidence against him
Faith in the Scottish legal system
Money well spent by the Establishment

Cure for the virus

MULAN'S FAIRY PRINCESS.

"Do you think Boris should have begun the clamp-down sooner?"
"Of course. It would have saved many more lives."

"Okay if I feel your arse today?"

THUNBERG

Only had corona virus for 50 minutes.
Only the good die young.

Morning, Chess-lovers

MY SON HAS BORROWED MY COMPUTER, SO I HOPE YOU CAN FORGIVE AN UNUSUAL NUMBER OF ERRORS IN THIS MONTH'S REPORT. FOR ONCE, MY NAME IS NOT AT THE TOP OF THE LEADER—BOARD, BUT MY PHOTO WILL APPEAR IN ALL THE LOCAL MAGAZINES AS NORMAL. YOUR SINCERELY,

Jonathan

Will Smith, tests negative!

For **bubonic plague.**

Tech by VICE

Health Officials Ask You to Please Masturbate, Because of Coronavirus.
"Kissing can spread COVID-19 and rimming might even spread it further," the NYC health department warns. We need to be told?

Government health warning, advising people to self-isolate...

By USULI TWELVES | Published: MARCH 29, 2020 | Edit

'Not clear enough, for party goers!" says Guardian stiff.

'WE OPERATE A GOOD NEIGHBOUR REPORTING SCHEME IN THIS AREA.'

Rogue Islander begins door to door checks for New Yorkers fleeing pandemic.

Protect our NHS

By SARIN | Published: MARCH 29, 2020 | Edit

"Saves lives"

"Bit of a moving feast"

"Government talking up numbers"

"People told to stay at home and not eat any flying rodents"

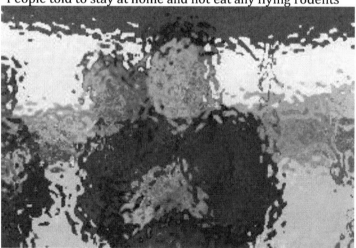

Look'n good, as a Health Service volunteer

A chance to get away from your boring partner

A free shag, whenever anyone isn't looking

Your name in the paper as a Saint and a Martyr

A chance to work alongside the great and the powerful

Added to your C.V. for a certain reward...

"How to dominate the world quickly? THE GREAT CHINESE STAGE 1. Create a virus and the antidote. 2. Spread virus. 3. A demonstration of efficiency, building hospitals in a few days. After all, you were already prepared, with the projects, ordering the equipment, hiring the labor, the water and sewage network, the prefabricated building materials and stocked in an impressive volume. 4. Cause chaos in the world, starting with Europe. 5. Quickly plaster the economy of dozens of countries. 6. Stop production lines in factories in other countries. 7. Cause stock markets to fall and buy companies at a bargain price. 8. Quickly control the epidemic in your country. After all, you were already prepared. 9. Lower the price of commodities, including the price of oil you buy on a large scale. 10. Get back to producing quickly while the world is at a standstill. Buy what you negotiated cheaply in the crisis and sell more expensive what is lacking in countries that have paralyzed their industries. PS: Read the book by Chinese colonels Qiao Liang and Wang Xiangsui, from 1999, "Unrestricted Warfare: China's Master Plan to Destroy America", on Amazon. It's all there. Worth pondering...just think about this. How come Russia and North Korea are totally free of Covid- 19? Because they are staunch allies of China. Not a single case reported from this 2 countries. On the other hand South Korea / United Kingdom / Italy / Spain and Asia are severely hit. How come Wuhan is suddenly free from the deadly virus? China will say that the drastic initial measures they took was very stern and Wuhan was locked down to contain the spread to other areas. I am sure they are using the Antidote for the virus. Why not Beijing? Why only Wuhan? Kind of interesting to ponder upon...right? Well...Wuhan is open for business now. America and all the above mentioned countries are devastated financially. Soon American economy will collapse as planned by China. China knows it CANNOT defeat America militarily as USA is at present the most powerful country in the world. So use the virus...to cripple the economy and paralyse the nation and its Defense capabilities. I'm sure Nancy Pelosi got a part in this...to topple Trump. Lately, President Trump was always telling of how GREAT American economy was improving in all fronts. The only way to destroy his vision of making AMERICA GREAT AGAIN is to create economic havoc. Nancy Pelosi was unable to bring down Trump thru impeachment, so work along with China to destroy Trump by releasing a virus. Wuhan's epidemic was a showcase. At the peak of the virus epidemic, China's President Xi Jinping...just wore a simple RM1 facemask to visit those effected areas. As President he should be covered from head to toe...but it was not the case. He was already injected to resist any harm from the virus...that means a cure was already in place before the virus was released. Some may ask...Bill Gates already predicted the outbreak in 2015...so the Chinese agenda cannot be true. The answer is...YES...Bill Gates did predict...but that prediction is based on a genuine virus outbreak. Now China is also telling everyone that the virus was predicted well in advance...so that it's agenda would play along well to match that prediction. China's vision is to control the world economy by buying up stocks now from countries facing the brink of severe economic collapse. Later, China will announce that their medical researchers have found a cure to destroy the virus. Now China have other countries stocks in their arsenal and these countries will soon be slave to their master...CHINA. Just Think about it ... The Doctor who declared this virus was also silenced by the Chinese authorities...and he didn't die from the virus, either. Is it overthinking? Or has it played out a bit too conveniently for China? You decide."

Sorry, Andy, I'm surprised you thought I'd appreciate such an aggressive and divisive diatribe! It's well-written but that's the only positive comment I can make. The Chinese whistle blower did die and Russia does have Covid-19, some people infected and some dead. They've been closing borders.

My daughter's partner is Chinese, so my grandchildren are half Chinese. I had previously been sent a beautiful image, a compassionate poem and two practical sets of advice, one on managing the virus at home and the other giving information about hygiene measures. They were my 'thing', though I can look up advice myself if I need to. Anyway, take care, Andy. love, Sally x

I don't know enough of the history, Andy, to make an informed comment but what I would say is that we are expert at exaggerating whatever scare there might be and leaving it to the media to turn into a panic. Best of all try to get The Speccy online using my reference RDK6MSQ6 00156 999. Don't miss Dr John Lee 28th. March page 24.

I'm not too worried about all this and take a daily constitutional for 45 minutes.

Happy solitude   Charles.

*They refused to pay out on my weekly lottery win at the supermarket tonight Charley boy. That's never happened before...!

≤ *You can have all our faulty equipment for keeps*

PIGS COLOUR WATER IN AN EFFORT TO DISCOURAGE WALKERS

THEY SHOULD NEVER HAVE GIVEN THEM THE COLOURING-IN BOOKS.

Hi Andy

I'm not too bad thanks...under the circumstances with these terrible times we live in. Yesterday I had a laptop delivered so that I can start working from home next week. It won't be easy for me with the job I do, but will just have to see how it goes. I take it you mean you've seen a picture of me playing Mr Badger...yes it was on the Sunday after the Whittlesford event. I really enjoyed Whittlesford and after winning both games on the Sunday actually finished joint first!! Had a thoroughly enjoyable evening match at Lowestoft the following night but then since then this virus has stopped all over the board chess following the Newmarket event. The event was a team event, however many teams pulled out in the days leading up to it. I found it difficult to concentrate to be honest...I did draw with a 186 in the morning but then played liked an idiot against 'the old Brock'!,,,that's my excuse anyway!! Where was the picture?...hopefully it was a reasonably good one! Heather did also play at Newmarket and I noticed she had a good win in one of her games. I hope you and your loved ones are keeping ok.

Take Care & Best Wishes – Steve

Dear Local Resident,

It is with regret, but a certain amount of glee, that I must reject your application to join the ranks of volunteers on this year's Roman dig.

YOURS SINCERELY,

PETER PURVY

TRUMP CAUSED THE VIRUS

By ADUMLA | Published: MARCH 30, 2020 | Edit

Tried to negotiate with a gleaming two-faced Dictator

Attempted to defend the world against Chinese domination

Spent too much time trying to improve the US economy

We first got the idea from Koontz...

Had to visit the docs today, it wasn't that important to me, but I was told it was urgent. Two young men outside dressed in space gear were treating the place like a nuclear plant. People love power, don't forget. A lot of people will like all this control. Yes, I have been to that Lidl. It is a good one. I keep writing the odd little e-mail to Tona, because I know the situation she is in. What if the Chinese got the idea from reading his book?? I know the very person to ask...Sally! My sister is harassing me at the moment and trying to get all the other bullies in the family involved. Am playing a few on-line games.
I can hear my mum calling she has no pyjamas. I just gave her a pair.

Who had the most to gain from Harvey Winestain's downfall?

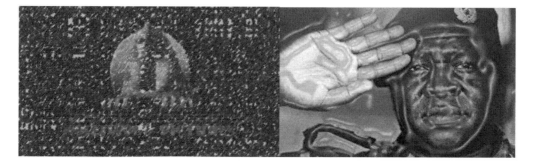

CHEAP, AT ANY PRICE

ITALY

By PETER SMITH | Published: APRIL 1, 2020 | *Edit*

"Puts Britain to shame."

Cleft child

By PETER SMITH | Published: APRIL 1, 2020 | *Edit*

Give them a chance to breed. Make sure they can smile.

HONESTY MORE IMPORTANT THAN KINDNESS.

Bramble Cottage Sanctuary and Rest-Home,

AYLSHAM,

Norfolk.

April 1/2020

Dear Mavis and David,

I'm writing to re-assure you all that my mum is being taken care of, and that she is safe and well, during this time of serious concern. I am doing everything I can to make life good for her, even though we can't mix like we used to. We are following the Government recommendations, and are self-isolating, although I am still able to take her out for a drive now and again.

A few days ago my mum took the telephone cord from the hallway, which connects the phone into a live socket. I am hoping to find it again. Until then I have offered to share my mobile phone with everyone, so they can speak to her, whenever convenient. All my sister has to do is give me a time and date, and I will make sure the phone is switched on and that she is ready to speak. You can always e-mail or write of course. I have also offered to set up a Skype account for her to use.

Genevieve says she has sent us a new phone, but my mum has no recollection of any delivery. Another point to bear in mind, is that my mum often fiddles with the phones, and there is nothing to stop it happening all over again. Mum gets angry if you ask her what she'd done with things.

As you may know, for the last few years I have been my mum's main carer. She has gradually grown more dependent on me, and is now at a stage where I don't think she could manage without me. I am looking after the home and garden as best I can, even though I have not been very well myself during the last few years. I consider it an honour and a privilege to be able to look after my mum in her old age.

I'm not saying it is always easy, but we do our best, and we do enjoy a reasonable amount of comfort and good humour most of the time. We get along better when there is no interference from other people. I'm afraid my sister seems to think she is monitoring both of us. The last time she was here she had an enormous row with my mum and swore she would never come back, after my mum accused her father of kicking her in the stomach when she was pregnant. My mum doesn't even know what her surname is, and neither of us were invited to her recent wedding. The last time I saw my sister she said I was "on my own from now on..." and that if anything ever happened to my mum I would have to get out of the house. She denied saying both these things the last time she was on the phone. Having got her hands on two properties, I suppose she is after a third.

The last time Aunty Jenny was here I asked her to leave the washing up for me to do, but she insisted she do it her own way. I asked her to let me manage the work, and that it felt as if she was interfering in our home. Uncle Kevin said Jenny was not interfering, which I suppose is just what you would expect him to say. I think it was the only time they spoke to me. It used to make me cringe the way he was so besotted with my sister she could never do any wrong. I would rather tell the truth than seek to be popular. Anyway, I hope you are all well up there. I do occasionally keep in touch with some old friends in the area, but haven't been back for years.

I HOPE YOU CAN READ MY TERRIBLE WRITING. Mum has hidden the phone again.

I did write to Swapper, but he said he was too busy counting all his money.

Visit from the Fuzz

By PETER SMITH *| Published: APRIL 1, 2020 | Edit*

We had a visit from the Fuzz today.   Two officers at our front door asking if we were self-isolating and breathing in our faces. It then emerged that the Butt had arranged for 'Swapper' to ring them, to see why we had not been answering the phone. He'd never bothered to ring for months. Had we had a delivery…?

I had explained why the wire was missing from the hallway, but the-Butt doesn't seem to understand anything about early stage dementia…

So, you have our new number. Why hasn't he rung?

As I turned to walk away, I heard mum whisper:

"I've something to tell you about Andrew…"

"You talk to me as if I'm a 'demented dwarf'…"

Belinda's late-night shoppers

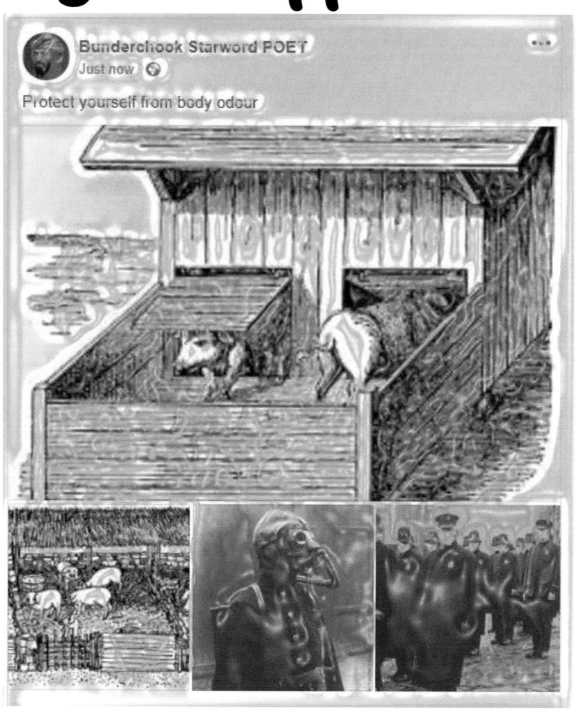

HEATHER

It's great to know you are doing so well on the cube.

Thanks for all your wonderful photos of the garden.

Jonathan posted a picture of himself as a youngster winning an award for chess. He says he retired from the game forty years ago, but there's no fooling us.

How is Magdalen Square these days?

In defence of the President by Usuli Twelves

On the face of it, the President's comments about injecting disinfectant straight into the body sound extremely dangerous and unpleasant, but there is some logic behind his thinking. He has obviously heard that disinfectant kills the virus, and was wondering if there was something in it which could be used to help cure the illness. No-one is seriously going to go immediately to the cupboard and start shooting this stuff straight into their blood stream. It's easy to make fun of someone, especially when they carry such a heavy responsibility and are coping with a lot of stress, at a time of great upheaval. Who could do any better than him, or provide greater statesmanship. Is there anyone who has been completely perfect in everything they say, all of the time? His slightly quirky and out -of-the-box way of thinking belies a caring nature, and someone who is trying desperately to think of ways that will genuinely improve the situation. I would still rather he was there, instead of a fake two-faced slick-talking Clinton. No-one can fault his sincerity in trying to contribute something. It was probably not the right choice of words, but then, Mr Trump is not a medical person. He was just trying to do his best.

Don't worry Mr. President. We know what you mean.

Donald Shipman Trump

By BIRD DUNG | Published: APRIL 24, 2020 | Edit
A great way to finish off your ailing relative…

NAKED FROM THE WAIST DOWN

So, you think me a clown,
For being naked,
From the waist down,
Trying on clothes,
In a fashionable town.

Is it a crime,
To be half naked, in your prime?
In the bathroom,
Or on a nudist beach...

But to be naked,
From the waist down,
In a changing-cubicle,
Just down the road,
Could land you in jail.

Dear Spectator (*Problem page*),

I've been sending material in to my local rag for a few years now with as much inappropriate content as I can muster. It mainly consists of poetry and short stories, but I have sometimes offered them the very odd landscape photograph. Not once have I received a single reply, not even to say they don't know me from Adam, yet the local Vicar gets a whole page to himself every issue.

His unashamed proselytizing always contains best wishes to everyone, the most sycophantic crap, peace and goodwill to men on earth, and a gleaming picture of himself in front of the chapel. I have written to the Editor to tell her that I am fed up of seeing so much faking wank in her magazine and that it makes me want to leave town and join a coven of witches. I had thought of offering her a bribe, but I'm not sure if I can keep going for as long as I used to mate.

My question is. Do you think I should change my poetic metre from iambic pentameter to anapestic, or re-educate myself at the right public school?

Bandits at eight o'clock, mi-lud. Has anyone seen Jeeves?

Shooting in Canada

By USULI TWELVES | *Published: APRIL 23, 2020* | *Edit*

Only 19 gunned down. Was he a poor shot?

Mavis 2

By PETER SMITH | *Published: MAY 1, 2020* | *Edit*

"Have you heard from Social Services yet?"
"No. Should we have done?"

If I die, on your conscience be it…

Justin from where?

Guard shot by shopper

I was there. He said; "Get that mask on and hide your ugly mug, or I'm going to shove your head so far down the nearest bog it will need an entirely different size of hat!"

Irish shit

By PETER SMITH | Published: MAY 10, 2020 | Edit

We were watching a film this morning. I started to tell the Little Shitzah about Stephen Boyd, who came from a small town called Glengormley in County Antrim.

"Irish shit," she replied.

TIME YOU WAXED THE MOUSTACHE
My Grandad always said they would...

By BIRD DUNG | Published: APRIL 21, 2020 | Edit

and they did!

The darkest times bring forth the greatest humanity...

Foxes Glacier Mints

By BIRD DUNG | Published: APRIL 21, 2020 | Edit

We had a little bust-up this morning about her taking all the milk from the fridge and leaving it in her room…

"What do you mean I'm not normal, you're the one who's not normal!"

A bit later I remembered a story Sally had told me about her mother, who kept putting Fox's Glacier mints into the cat's food bowl. They still had their paper on.

In an attempt to lighten the mood, I told mum about this. I asked her what she thought of it.

Mum stared towards me: "Did she eat them?"

My wonderful nosey neighbours

By BIRD DUNG | Published: APRIL 14, 2020 | Edit

Out exercising in the garden today and self-isolating, due to the pandemic. It was a lovely sunny day, so I was in my swimming trunks. I had a sudden feeling of Deja vu, as the mechanical whirr of a helicopter appeared on the horizon. It sped directly towards me at top speed, and circled overhead.

"Stupid old git!"

R E J E C T E D

e-harmony

You stuck your head on a super-hero's body!

Bure Valley Margaret

By RUMPLESTILTSKIN | Published: MAY 5, 2020 | Edit

Bure Valley Margaret saw me enter the supermarket from the wrong direction today. There was no-one else in the queue, so I asked the doorman if it was alright if I came in that way. As I went inside, I saw her rush back and start telling him the lies she is famous all-round town for. I couldn't help noticing the smirk written all across her face.

I told him not to listen to her. He was a big lad, but made of blub, and about one third my age.

He said; "you need to have respect for women."

I said; "this has nothing to do with having respect for women."

He said; "there's no need to be like that."

I said; "have you ever thought of joining the fuzz...ah, too bright I suppose..."

"I made no mention of the fact that she is a former prostitute, or that she was once arrested for shoplifting.

NB See. This is where I've grown weak. The old me would have said...."so, I don't respect them. What are you going to do about it you little cunt?"

Tesco trolls with arm-bands

By PETER SMITH | Published: MAY 6, 2020 | Edit

Reprimanded today;
1 Asking to leave my mountain bike outside the door
2 Returning my basket in an improper manner
3 Walking forward without the correct authority

"You are my last hope. If anything goes wrong with you that will be the end for me." BASEMA October 2006

Hi Denise! Step-sister.

I don't feel as if I can visit my GP anymore. went to the grave. mum wouldn't get out of the car so I got out on my own and picked some wild flowers. she threw my mints all over the floor while I was gone. I actually felt very moved walking up the path to your dad. Xx

Hi Mavis!

I was only trying to tell you the land-line phone wasn't working again, and to give you my new mobile number, before the phone went dead. I wondered if there was any way you could ask Swapper not to call the cops on us again.

Dinner at the Savoy Deli

Loyal Biden supporters attempt to prevent his arrest on false assault charges. He's being accused of planting his finger in an *uncomfortable spot* 27yrs ago, when he really meant to point at the window. The President rang his main rival to ask how wet or dry it was.

Join the Chinese Communist party or else...

Get your ass over that hill. I'll show you how to tame the virus!

IN THE GARDEN

Message sent by Elizabeth Farley-hills: 'I love you dearly. Shall we get married?' (Not long before her application for an ASBO).

LADY-OF-PLEASURE., SEEKING PART-TIME BAR-WORK PULLING YOUR KNOB

Dear Mari,

Thank you for your recent letter which contained a copy of my Will. I hope you received my payment which I sent in the post. I have been under a lot of stress since my husband died and have found it hard to manage sometimes.

Although I am aware of a previous Will, which was made under pressure from my daughter, I am adamant that the wishes expressed in this new Will, be upheld. I am perfectly capable of making this decision on my own, even though I aren't getting any younger and I'm getting crazier by the minute.

I have been assessed for Alzheimer's at my Doctors, and was found not to be suffering from it. A few months ago, I did answer a few questions from the Doctor at the Market Surgery concerning my awareness and capability, and he seemed perfectly content with my answers. He asked me my name, the date, and my son's name, which is Kevin.

I still do not think my daughter will contest the will as it makes generous and adequate provision for her children, but there again, she is a greedy cow.

I am quite happy for a Doctor to witness my re-signing at some point in the future. Do you really think it necessary for me to get a professional care-consultant. How long would the interview last? I would need help to set up an internet connection at my home. £500 pounds is quite a lot of money to some people. *Sincerely,* **The Little Shitzah**

V

"Andy 'hard-on'"

For those of you unfamiliar with Hollywood history: Mickey Rooney met Ava Gardner on a film-set shortly after she arrived through the gates. He had been starring in a series called 'Andy Hardy.' Gardner was only eighteen, and still a virgin. Something which Rooney swore to put right on their wedding night. She was already considered to be the most beautiful woman in the world. This was in the days when you could charm an aspiring actress on the audition couch without having to explain why you whipped your cock out.

Rooney walked up to Gardner and used his by now standard chat-up line;

"I wanted to fuck you the first time I set eyes on you..." A nice kind little man with ginger hair and freckles.

He was nick-named 'Andy Hard-on' by one of his previous conquests, Lana Turner, who confessed in her memoirs that Rooney had an ambition to shag every good-looking female in the studio, and that he had come very close to fulfilling his goal.

Gardner went on to marry Howard Hughes, who she said "wouldn't piss on a black man to put him out, if he was on fire." Charming.

Nice choice in men love!

Eddie Chapman double-act

She thought he looked like Winston Churchill

Completely unlike our Kevin of course. We were watching a documentary about a chap who had been a womaniser, a cheat, and a complete villain during the Second world war. He used everyone he met to make himself rich and didn't have a shred of guilt or remorse about the people he had trampled on. I said look mum! It's Kevin. His real name was Douglas Chapman, and he lived in Norfolk around that time.

MARE QUARE: DOESN'T LOOK HAPPY

YOU HOPE AND PRAY FOR YEARS FOR A VIRUS TO COME ALONG AND ERADICATE THE SICK OLD PARASITES FROM SOCIETY. AND WHEN IT DOES, THEY TRY TO KILL IT.

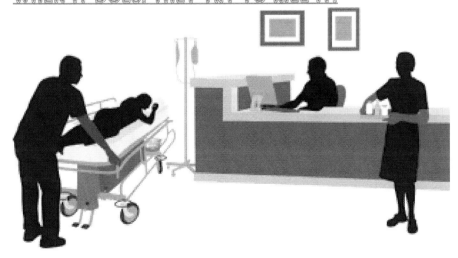

UK Government say….

By BIRD DUNG | Published: MAY 4, 2020 | Edit

"Test, track and chase! We will do our very best to protect your freedom and ease this terrible lock-down."

Plane over-head

By SARIN | Published: MAY 7, 2020 | Edit

A white aeroplane was circling over the garden today. The pilot came round at least three times. I imagine he was saying to his passenger/s:
"Hey, see the red head on him!"
I urged the Little Shitzah to keep her foul tongue quiet, when we came into the garden today;
"Just in case Janet is out."

The terrible Jelly-man

By SARIN | Published: MAY 7, 2020 | Edit

I had an e-mail the other day from my old college chum, who I had talked out of his obsession long ago. He still insists on sending me flowers and a card each spring, in memory of the time I stopped him from buying his twelve-year-old neighbour a box of chocolates and a rain-jacket.

Fashion accessories

182

Dear Mavis (and *David*),

As promised, I've made sure my mum speaks to you ever few days so you can hear how well she is doing. I hope you are alright, and that your scan has turned out okay.

We had our meals outside today, it was so nice. She usually wears a hat because she is very sensitive to the sun. She ate quite well, but then she was very tired. I've just cleaned all-round the house, including the conservatory, with the help of a very long brush.

I am including a picture of her taken today when we were outside, with her new Zimmer, which she loves, and has adapted to very well. She's never had one in her life, but has been getting a lot of discomfort in her knee. It helps her to balance, but unfortunately it will not do much to reverse her insanity.

I do hope nothing I say will be used against me. I like to be frank with people. You asked me if we had been contacted by Social Services. As I replied to you on the phone: my sister Genevieve tried to get them involved about two years ago and my mother didn't want them here. I find my sister very controlling and arrogant. We don't need to be managed, supervised, or monitored, by her, or anyone else. We are doing alright by ourselves, and do not need strangers coming into the house and taking over. Any friend of Genevieve's, or who has been listening to her spurious stories about me, is certainly no friend of mine.

My mum seems very settled, living here in her own home, and being cared for by me.

If we need to have Social Services involvement, we will ring them ourselves. I did speak to them myself about a year or so ago, but decided there was nothing they could offer us. I'm very disappointed with Uncle Bobby (Swapper) sending the police round on us because we hadn't answered the phone. As I explained; this was due to a wire going missing. He hadn't bothered to ring for months anyway. As I said before; what's wrong with writing or sending an e-mail? You could say he was easily manipulated by my sister, but then he must have been willing to go along with it too. Mum took the phone again the other day, and I couldn't find where it was. I don't think things will ever be the same again. We are quite lucky here. We have a very comfortable life and plenty of resources. I would hate to live in one of the big cities during this futile lock-down. On the positive side; restrictions are going to be slowly lifted. Then we will be able to visit more shops and travel further afield.

1 Please tell Uncle Bobby that there is no need to organise any more welfare checks on us.

2 As you know, my mum's behaviour was always very strange on occasions.

Yours, lovingly, BLUNDERCHOOK

Comments

NO COMMONERS BEFORE MID-DAY...

Social Services

Dear Occupant,

I am writing to inform you that you have been allocated a Social Worker. This follows your visit from the police over two weeks ago. Next Thursday I will be calling to see you with a male member-of-staff, who will assess your son's unsuitability for Care-work.

We are not interested in why the police called, or whether your phone line was faulty. What really matters is your label.

Your daughter has rung us several times to get you admitted into a home.

One of your neighbours has also told us that she heard shouting in the garden.

If you continue to defend your son and say he is an excellent Carer, then we will have no option but to file a false and twisted record of our conversation.

Bel Kauin, is here to say,

Write your poem and go away,

When you're gone I'll sing my song,

While sitting on my lavatory.

Teachers refuse to go back to govern lazy unruly pupils

By RUMPLESTILTSKIN | Published: MAY 16, 2020 | Edit

Ah, in need of a pay rise. Too much free time chatting to your work colleagues on your smart-phone.

Rich countries who made the vaccine not allowed to benefit

By SARIN | Published: MAY 17, 2020 | Edit

'Rich' countries, who have ploughed resources into creating a vaccine, for the virus created in a lab, or festered in the bat's wings sold on the open market....should not be allowed to profit, say human rights campaigners and charity workers helping to promote a rise in the poor African population...

SHE FINALLY GOT HER BLACK

Dear Barclays,

I am an eighty-four-year-old woman needing help and assistance. I am quite frail at the moment and unable to access your on-line facilities which I find extremely confusing. I have tried to ring on the phone countless times and have found the whole experience very time-consuming and exasperating. My local bank has been closed and I cannot get to a bank on foot.

I would like to know:

1 Has there been an amount of about £90 refunded from my car insurance with Age UK? This would have been around March time this year.

2 I noticed in my recent statement that an amount of £196 pounds had been taken out of my account. I would like to know if my daughter has been sneaking money out again.

3 On a visit to the bank some months ago the Manager was with me when we destroyed my Barclaycard, as it was no longer required. I have just been sent a statement saying I am owed £139.98 which I would like transferring into my currant account please.

"Hello, China City...?"

"Speak your order please."

"Sweet and sour bat wings, a curried rat, and four boiled monkeys in a bag."

MARRIOTT'S WAY

So many times,
Along the disused railway line,
Scurrying into the undergrowth,
Or stopping to look at me from your space craft,
Until that day you came to visit,
sprawled in front of the winter flame.
You rolled about on the carpet,
Displaying your long whiskers,
Pawing at my leg,
Leaving an impression.
But you never returned from the ether,
Even though we sent out search parties,
To look for you in the heather.
All over the moor we trooped,
And thought we saw you,
Sometimes running,
In the distance.

Yes, thank you, though I lost both my games last night against Andy Hartland (ECF 157A). They were good games though, and the chess.com stats for the first game said he played it with 98.0% accuracy, so not much I could do against that! The second game was going well for me and he said he couldn't find a move, but he soon did when I blundered and let his bishop fork my rooks. So that was the end of that K
Never mind, Broadland won the match 6-4. Since then I've been badgering round a lot in the garden.

I thank you for your belated acknowledgement of my brilliance!

You may have beaten me by a few positions in the blitz, but I came first in this one! I thrashed Allan Holmes after the fiftieth time of asking...he gave in. Haha!
I'm playing in the Norfolk Live Classic Arena tonight against Stephen Livermore, ECF 107A, so I stand absolutely no chance there!
Have a great day, yes, I think it's going to be a good one.

Love from Heather x

RUTA. It had been on my mind to write to you again for a while and I was just anticipating what to say when your message came in. Yes, there was something on the news. Some people went to Weybourne, nearby... and left bags of rubbish on the beach....with disgusting things inside.

You and Virginija are both very sociable people. her even more than you I think.

I still find trouble sleeping, but then when I do get up I have jobs to do, painted the garage door, trimmed the hedges, made mum her dinner.

do you remember when we used to go to the park in North Walsham, and that fair when it was there. mad place. we walked up many different levels, to the top of a crazy house. haha!

Bacton woods are supposed to be nice. also, down by Blickling Hall. I have cycled through there and it is beautiful. I know lots of beautiful places up in Yorkshire. I went on my cycle ride up Marriotts Way again today. if only you had a bike. you wouldn't believe the wonderful countryside around. Its even better going up from Norwich. I don't watch a lot of telly, but when I do I love to watch nature programmes, where you can imagine the fresh air against your cheeks.

I can see how Rokas and Erikas will find social distancing very difficult when they go back to school, as one day they must. I am sad to think you are not very happy. Life has its ups and downs. One day you will be happy again I promise. Do you ever collect any wild flowers when you are in the woods. we used to press flowers in a book when we were young.

Yep. been through a lot a few years ago. got involved with the wrong woman. that's partly why I am poorly sometimes now. I always used to be able to count on my physical strength to get me through, but now I am old. a lot older than you, anyway. lol.

I kinda gave up trying years ago. I don't even bother to smarten up any more. I saw Virginija look down at my boots. I hadn't even be bothered to tie the laces properly.

I've seen her on a dating site a few times over the last few years. I used to look at them even when I was with Christine. good luck to her. I always remember that day on the railway, where the man bumped into her by mistake from behind and her hand reached up instinctively between his legs...

"What are testicles?" she asked me. Er, she is a nurse.

Anyway. mum is safely tucked in bed. am eating liver for supper. I did quite well in my last two tournaments on line. was well ahead of Heather in a blitz at the weekend.

Chess is only a bit of fun for me. I try not to take it too seriously and don't have the inclination to go through all my games like some people do... I am more interested in art and literature...

still keeping myself fit pumping weights in the garden.

She's found a boy-friend? That explains everything.

Dear Ruta,

You are right. I am sure I could offer you something tastier for dinner than my liver.

What a strange dream you had, but not as strange as some of the ones I've had.

I did not mind explaining about testicles to Virgan (her dating site name).

It was only when I thought about it later that I found it at all unusual, her being a nurse
and everything. I have a lot of experience in life.

The best way to meet someone genuine is to be introduced by a mutual friend.

To anyone using these sites I would say; be very careful. A lot of them are fakes.

I thought it might have been you who took the photo she has on there!

Yes, I like having a bit of fun too. I could write a book about it... Virginija looked worn out in town, with bags round her eyes...So, she's happy,
now she has a boyfriend. I know of several women who were promised great sex by African men, in return for money and an air-ticket.

Our new Carer is already up-the-duff.

She did some shopping while we were out.

I expected to see a lot of things for the baby when I glanced in her bag.

All I could see where packets of sweets, potato crisps, and haribo.

Ariana Grande

By GODFREY WINKLEBACKER | Published: MAY 22, 2020 | Edit
A 'victim' of the Manchester Arena bombing said of its perpetrators today;

"I can't wait to spit on their grave!"

Gay man shot his load in parking lot while trying to swallow large gherkin...

The agony of living with bound feet: Chinese woman, 84, reveals how her feet were broken and bound when she was just six years old:

A Chinese woman has revealed how she endured having her feet bound when she was only six years old, even though the painful procedure had been outlawed.
Wang Huiyuan, now 84, who lives in the rural Tonghai County, Yunnan, had the 'beauty treatment' in the 1930s, decades after it had been officially banned in 1902.
'Then it was fashionable to bind feet. Everyone did it. If not, you'd be laughed at, "look at her big, flat feet". Once I was laughed at, I bound my feet,' she explained, 'But it still didn't stop us breeding like flies.'

Had her arse slapped...
By PETER SMITH | Published: MARCH 6, 2021 | Edit

Is Susie Dent really as nice as she seems.

Wrong gender, Colin!

Comings and goings

By <u>GODFREY WINKLEBACKER</u> | *Published: MAY 24, 2020* | *<u>Edit</u>*

It's a pity a parent can't drive hundreds of miles across country to protect their children without the press hounding them to death because they broke the rules, but if your name is Dominic Cummings and you were the mastermind behind the Brexit campaign, then this will continue until they have you out of your job, they hope. You can tell the rabble the truth til you're blue in the face Mr. Prime-Minister, but they will still find fault with his actions because they want to damage the Government. The truth is not something they are ever likely to want to hear. According to the two-faced pompous hypocritical British press it is wrong to go on your instincts. Take my advice Dominic. Tell them all to buzz off!

LAW MAKERS, LAW BREAKERS!

Comments

"I've a good mind to resign if it will make me look smart!"

Asked to take it down

By <u>GODFREY WINKLEBACKER</u> | *Published: MAY 24, 2020* | *<u>Edit</u>*

I was asked to take my profile picture of Adolf Hitler down, prior to our chess match with the Berlin Bishops. The manager of my team thought it might get me kicked off the site and it would save a lot of hassle, if it upset anyone. I suppose it would be no good reminding a *staunch member of the Establishment* about the importance of the 'right to offend?' He's a sweet little guy who reminds me of my old college chum. Yes, you've guessed it! The onerous Jelly-man. Matt has many of the tiny persistent mannerisms he had, but without the venom and naturally evasive circumlocution. I have a hunch, although nothing to do with bell-ringing, that a stickler for the law, like Heather, probably snitched on me. I replaced the picture with one of the Fat-man, which quickly disappeared a few moments later. Stephen Hawking has the lime-light now, but shortly before the contest I intend to replace him with one of General Ludendorff...

"Governments talk shit!"

AN ACT OF REBELLION

Deliberately put my shirt on inside out this morning, before breakfast and trolling round the house. A little later I ventured outside to retrieve the bin, and bumped into my neighbour, Janet, forgetting all about it.

When I went back inside I suddenly realised what I had done, and went back to talk to her.

"You didn't tell me I had my T-shirt inside out, did you!" I said.

"It was back to front as well," she pondered.

At least I did not make any improper sexual innuendo concerning her off-spring.

Swedish Prime-minister says:-

HARD LINES IF YOU ARE GRAY

GRAVE ROBBERS

A £10,000 fine for going to the pub (but only if you are 'disobedient,' orders the **House of Lords**).

Smoothing the waves

While the Barn-owl decides,
She's smoothing the waves,
Folding the sheets,
   And returning the heat.

Talking out loud,
   To the cat and the clouds,
As the pale Moon descends,
Through the evening shroud.

Again and again,
   The changes are made,
Searching her bag,
And covering the bed,
Hanging her coat,
On the lamp-shade nearby,
Drowning poor Sam,
In a mountain of pee.

Dear Kindle,

I hope we can sort this problem out together. I have been with you for many years, and before that, Create-Space. I was always immensely happy with our relationship. I have always found the staff to have a very positive attitude and they have always tried to help. I would be extremely saddened to lose it and have all my work removed.

I am also a long term loyal customer of Amazon. I buy almost everything from this company, before anyone else.

I was told by a member of the Kindle staff some time ago that if I did use an image from the Internet it would be alright as long as I distorted it or made it different. Many of my images are my own creation, or from paintings and photos of my own.

It would be a shame to destroy so much great writing, when the images are really only secondary, only used as a pun.

I could easily remove them or completely destroy the current file.

The book, or book(s) under review were titled: Bunderbuck Starbird Phoenix 'regeneration,' Ethical Cleansing.

ASIN: B08HTJ7BN2
ASIN: B086BB48YQ

I thank you for your support.

'Man is a wonderful, kind and humane creature!'

ONCE LEFT IN EVERY BEDROOM

Dear Doc Gillam,

I really can't come in to the surgery labelled as a Sex-offender.
I would like to know; for what (and when??).
When I told you about the treatment I received from the Quakers (after one of their senior members had gone running off to the pigs, and to *another* church in the town) you appeared to be sympathetic towards them.
I'm sorry I was unable to take your call as I do not carry a phone around with me all the time.
I wanted to talk to a Doctor about:
1 A pimple under my left testicle caused by riding my bike.
2 The pains and numbness I keep getting on the left side of my head.

I spoke to a receptionist today who found the whole subject extremely amusing.

•

YOURS SINCERELY,

A CATFISH

NO BADGERS.

A great sunny one again. yep. have had a few problems playing on line, but decided not to take it too seriously. its not chalked up about five of my recent games as victories or added to my number of heads, but who cares. I know. that's what counts. I only just signed in today, and was too late for the Essex one I think. am due to play next week I thought. 1st June already!!! Don't get too upset when it crashes. it probably happens to a lot of people, but very annoying when it's in the middle of a tight game.

I mentioned not believing in 'duty' a while back. may sound like a contradiction. I tend to act with a sense of duty, but that is because of my 'conditioning.' doing the right thing etc. but as a concept, I would have no problem disobeying orders if someone said it was my duty to shoot someone. I look after my mum because I think it's the right way to behave. it is for me, anyway.

sending one or two pics taken today of my daily cycle route along part of Marriott's Way which runs past my house. Sorry to hear Keith called round when you were busy on your cubes. He told me Paul had been badgering him to play for Broadland.

Hope you had a good one. see you again one day soon. How about pinning a sign on your door?

"When the King decides to disembowel you try not to let him see you are in pain…"

Biden in secret deal with Antifa

By PETER SMITH | Published: JUNE 3, 2020 | Edit

1. Make this an issue about race and not police brutality
2. Keep the pressure on Trump and hope that he will crack
3. Maintain that 'black lives matter' more than yellow
4. Stir up the crowd and blame in on the President
5. Persist with the ignorant idea of equality for all
6. Offer bribes to the media barons
7. Hope that by throwing enough mud some of it will stick

Elizabeth Rigsby

By Albert R. Swipe | Published: MAY 28, 2020 | Edit

Bit of a Laura Kuentzberg.

Oxford legal Secretary

By BIRD DUNG | Published: MAY 31, 2020 | Edit
"You have a lot of problems…"
"Thanks for letting me know."
"Is that why you let them confiscate all my poetry books…"

Disproportionately affected by the shit-heads

By Bubba Hardfat | Published: JUNE 1, 2020 | Edit
"If we don't do something soon, the population will go on growing indefinitely!"

Media continues to stir up trouble for Trump

By USULI TWELVES | Published: JUNE 3, 2020 | Edit

Twisting everything he says
Encouraging rioters to break the law
Fuelling the frenzy

Blaming him for the deaths of half a million Americans

Praising the piss out of Joe Biden

Veuillez nous protéger de notre police

SHOW SOME LOVE FOR YOUR FELLOW MAN

TAKE EVERYTHING YOU CAN BEFORE THEY GET HERE

Grand Goblin of the invisible Empire

By SARIN | Published: JUNE 9, 2020 | Edit

The time has come for us to make an urgent appeal to members of the public. Our membership has been falling for a significant number of years, but we hope to recruit many new members in the coming months. Membership is on an ad hoc basis, with fees paid up front and donated to our royal band of fire-starters.

St. George Floyd

By USULI TWELVES | Published: JUNE 9, 2020 | Edit

Armed robbery

Pointing a gun at a pregnant female

Assaulting a police officer

Resisting arrest

Offering drugs to a primary school

Bag handler

Pimping the arm of the law

Saying; "Just wait till I get up from here. "

"I'm gonna make you sorry you even had a knee!"

"Hallelujah! Praise the Lord!"

Dear Social Services,

My mum, Mrs. Margaret Amis, has informed me that you contacted her. May I first of all thank you for your kind concern and for your offer of support. It's nice to know that there are caring people in the community who are ready to respond quickly and who can help when someone is finding life difficult to cope with.

I have been looking after my mum for about five years now, during which time we have had one or two ups and downs. Most families do at some point. It's not easy looking after old people as you know, which is why my long experience of caring for people is so invaluable: I worked as an Instructor in Occupational therapy for a number of years and also as a live-in Carer and Companion in Oxford for four years. I have also worked as a supervising manager in a Residential home for older people. The relationship with my mother has actually improved since I began caring for her. I have become her closest friend and companion after spending many years away from her, living my own life.

My mum has started to depend on me more as the years have gone by. She expects me to make her meals, to look after the house and gardens, do her laundry, and to take her shopping each week (she no longer drives). I recently bought her a Zimmer-frame, which she has never had before, because her knee was sore again, and she was having difficulty walking. She has adapted to it very well, although she only uses it when she really needs to. We are self-isolating at the moment, so we can't go out very much. We both value our privacy, and just want to live a quiet life, without being harassed by anyone.

My mum sometimes takes things and puts them in a drawer, and then forgets where they are. This has been happening for a long time. She has removed the phone more than once.

Unfortunately, I haven't always got on with my sister. I find her a bit authoritarian and very bossy. The last time she was here she had an enormous row with my mum, and told me she would never come back again and didn't want anything more to do with her. After that she did ring occasionally from abroad, but I told her we didn't need monitoring by her. I told her that a wire had gone missing from the hall, which linked the phone to the socket, but that things usually turned up eventually. My sister is able to e-mail me every day, to Skype, and to write by post. She also has my mobile number.

It was her idea to ask my uncle to phone the police when she couldn't get through. My uncle has not tried to phone my mother for months. I read the police a letter I had posted to my aunty explaining all of this. My mum was very stressed by the visit. Also, the police came without any masks or protection on, during the peak of the corona-virus out-break, and were breathing in our faces. I was very worried for my mother's sake.

A few years ago, I had some problems with an ex-partner, but this has all been finished with ages ago. My sister is always trying to bring up the past. She doesn't seem to have anything positive to say about me due to the whiteness of my skin.

I told the police that I considered it an honour to be able to look after my own mother in her old age. My mum has told me several times that she is happy with me caring for her and that she wants to stay in her own home, without my sister Genevieve forcing her to live in a home full of strangers.

I hope this puts you better in the picture and that we can communicate again, if ever aid was needed. I did get in touch with Social Services myself a couple of years ago trying to find what was available if we ever needed any extra help. I was of the opinion that you provided Care Assistants, but this proved not to be the case.

PAYLSHAM INTIMIDATION SERVICES

A reasonable offer for your business:

1. One used jam-jar
2. A box of tic-tacks
3. Seven yards of knicker elastic
4. A second-hand hand-loom
5. Some old boxing gloves
6. A roman candle
7. A variety of Standard fire-works
8. One un-lit paper taper
9. Two half-eaten custard pies

SO MUCH FOR ALL THE NEW FACE-RECOGNITION CAMERAS

You dirty clowns

Hi Roger,

Had been meaning to have a look at your chart again. A lot of what I said before will still apply but there is still a bit more to add. I'm basing it more on your natal and progressed charts than on any transits at the moment. Sorry I can't say any more, but when you do get a definite date for the hearing let me know. He's telling me you have kept his old watch, lying in a drawer at home...

I think your clear thinking and intelligence is always going to be an asset whenever you are in any kind of trouble. You have a good understanding of people which always helps you in any situation, although you may have a tendency to want to rush to get things done in a hurry. There still seems to be a lot of frustration around, with things repeating themselves over and over again, and not getting properly sorted out. With three planets retrograde, including Mars and Pluto, in Gemini, there may be a lot of disruption, but with possible new ways of interaction. You should always be able to find new ways of over-coming challenges.

There continues to be a delay in reaching a final decision, feeling energy is being wasted and that you are being restrained from getting things done. It's important for you to have your say, but sometimes you feel as if your words are being cut short. The power of Government and Authority seem to be stifling your freedom, and it feels like they are working against your goals, leaving some issues unresolved. Sometimes you get forced to accept responsibility for things which don't appear to be your fault, (although your friend was very accurate with the information you gave her about me).

There's a need for close contact with loved ones and the desire to be loved. You will experience some joyful fun times with kids, but they will be short lived. Trying to maintain relationships is something you keep attempting to do but sometimes you may feel a bit vulnerable, especially when people keep blaming you for things and letting you down.

You could still be a bit touchy and sensitive around this time. You are more guarded and defensive than normal. Sometimes you may feel deceived by others which makes you behave differently. It's difficult for you to know what to trust in at the moment. Sometimes it may feel as if the carpet has been pulled from under your feet, but stay positive. Things are about to improve. You will meet a gypsy on the road who will make you very rich. Your legs will give you more space when flying.

You asked me to be candid about what happened to me; while I was inside I noticed a file on the table in front of me. I was being interviewed by a right Jack-the-lad, who went under the name of 'Clinical Psychiatrist.' They can call themselves anything they like in there. It said on the cover of the file: <u>RAPIST: dangerous to women and children.</u> When I asked him why that was written on there, the best explanation he could come up with, was that I had been seen by Benji from the top of the stairs, locking the outside door, in 2007. One of the women spreading malicious rumours around town about me was in the zoom meeting you held. Roger? Where have you gone.....? Is anybody there?

- I COULDN'T HELP NOTICING HOW MUCH YOUNG FANNY YOU HAD KNOCKING AROUND IN THAT LITTLE CUL-de-SAC. A FEW OF THEM gATHERED NEAR THE PLAY AREA WATCHING ME AND SCRATCHING THEIR C...TS AS I LEFT.

SPIRITS ONLY TELL THE TRUTH

Geraldine (famous crime-writer). I thought you might like this:

RAFFERTY

I knew you would take it in good spirit. I've just heard. Is it true? You've been shortlisted for a top award.

Man discovered living only 50mls from a victim

Exploit at will

Female Copper knocked from horse by traffic light ends up on arse/bike thrown at horse

By PETER SMITH | Published: JUNE 7, 2020 | Edit
It was better in the good old days when all you needed was a lance.

DISGRACEFUL INEQUALITY

By PETER SMITH | Published: JUNE 7, 2020 | Edit
Anyone born in a particular place, at a certain time, and with webbed feet, will be affected by it for the rest of their adult life...

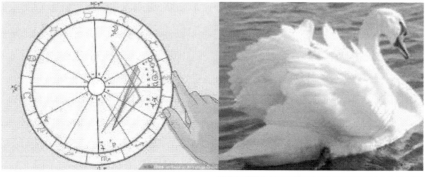

Hi

What did you tell them? Very interesting. People love to gossip or to talk about others.
I found Rokas notebook and he wrote a story long time ago about you and Virginija. It was very funny to read. He mentioned that you helped her with her course and that everybody says that Virginija is clever. But actually she is not clever as she needs help from you and others and he mentioned that you shook your boobs and it looked silly and clumsy. And he mentioned so many details: what song you listened and what you said..that he saw you sliding your hand into her jeans.
I am fine, sitting at home, watching TV and days passes so quickly.
I went to London on Tuesday because my passport expired. So nothing exciting. RUTA

'Iz it cos I'z black?'

OWN WHO YOU ARE *Be proud of where you come from...!*

GOOD THINGS TO KNOW ABOUT SLAVERY

Free food and lodgings if you do as you are told
Secure career advancement into your dog-kennel
Part of a team dedicated to preserving the status quo
Knowing you are appreciated by your Lords and Masters
A wide variety of social contacts among the sick and injured
Privileged and able to vote if you are lucky enough to write
A close relative of the rats clawing and scratching over your head

TAKE DOWN MY STATUE

Reaction of the Little Shitzah at having the wall painted yellow

By ADUMLA | Published: JUNE 8, 2020 | Edit

- ✓ Slamming of doors
- ✓ Spitting, shouting, punching, stamping the floor and hissing
- ✓ "Just wait till I show them what you've done!"

In the wrong way...

By BIRD DUNG | Published: JUNE 13, 2020 | Edit

Rebuked again for going in a supermarket the wrong way round.

"But, I'm dyslexic!"

It's official!

By Ginger Tom | Published: JUNE 14, 2020 | Edit

Government think-tank concludes that the disproportionately high number of black and Asian people dying of the virus is due to 'racism.' Reports BBC News-reader on behalf of all fair-minded and influential teachers working in our classrooms.

"Why can't you keep your damned legs together for more than five minutes?"

NOT BLOODY LIKELY

A bit of gardening

By Curly Burton | Published: JUNE 14, 2020 | Edit

I spoke to Eileen last night. We speak quite often, although I am trying to discourage her from using phrases like:

"I haven't had it for ages..."

and...

"Where would you like to put your hand tonight darling?"

'I've got to be honest,' I said. 'I like a woman to look like a woman. I don't like this new fashion of trimming the bush.'

"If you want a nice big hairy bush, you shall have one!" she laughed.

"Are you a Shower, or a Grower?"

"I'm a Shower WHEN I'm a Grower!" I said.

Pugly

GOT HIM!

Bring those shopping trolleys in will you

BLACK POWER MATTERS

Dear Tom/Mr Mayhew, As we are in communication, I thought of mentioning another small matter. I think it's important that our MP's understand what is going on in our world (if they don't already). My Mother, who is nearly 85, and suffers from confusion, is getting continuously harassed by Barclaycard. I spoke to them yet again yesterday, and explained everything carefully: My mum has not had a computer or been on the Internet in years. She has not had a Barclaycard or used one in years (her previous card was destroyed in front of the Manager at Aylsham years ago). The two false transactions from two Internet security companies were being investigated by their fraud dept. but we never heard back. Our letters were never answered. When we tried to talk to the Internet companies we could not get through security and they put the phone down on us. The two Asian gentlemen I spoke to at Barclaycard (who sounded very similar to the men who tried to scam money out of my mum's account, about two years ago), seemed to treat it all as a big joke, when I handed the phone over, so they could speak to her. They rang again repeatedly today. Is there anyone in this country who has a clue what to do about these Arseholes?

Fat-man with poor aim misses legitimate target

By PETER SMITH | Published: JUNE 15, 2020 | Edit

A man caught short on a London street missed his target by a mile, thereby saving himself a further month in custody. Don't forget your glasses next time. You are a bluddy disgrace!

PHOTO OPPORTUNITY

PELOSI DECLARED INSANE!

YOU'RE SUCH A PAIN

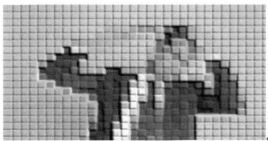
Joe looks great in his new face-mask…!

John Bolton, couldn't get a hard-on

By SARIN | Published: JUNE 19, 2020 | Edit

Spent most of his career sharpening his pencil

Sat on the john thinking of new ways to spike the President's coke

Twisted everything Mr Trump said in a bid for fame and glory

Peeved at being dumped in the trash after falling asleep at his desk

Felt let-down after a life-time of grease-balling

Angry that his duplicity and double-crossing nature had been compromised

Was secretly employed by Obama clones working for the Chinese Government

Went snivelling to the press about re-election details

Said that a one-track mind and plenty of dirt was needed, to get his book published

Thought that Trump should be impeached for nuclear espionage

Highly critical of the President for standing up for American interests abroad

Gave classes in how to take the mick out of his boss

PROTECT THE PRESIDENT   HILARY'S LOOKING FOR A MAN.

Had an Asian sounding gentleman on the phone this afternoon notifying me that a foreign bank, located somewhere just north of Manningham Lane, near the taxi-rank, had just tried to take £600, out of my account. It sounded genuine, that's why, like an absolute knob-head, I gave him my date of birth when he asked for it. I tried to get through to my bank on-line, but it was an absolute nightmare. They tried to scam me about a year ago and almost got away with two and a half grand. I surmise, they must have kept some of my personal details. If only we had a house number; I feel sure it would never happen again.

'My life was utterly ruined by Wind-rush'

Michael Jackson gave money to strangers

By GODFREY WINKLEBACKER | Published: JUNE 22, 2020 | Edit
Always said he was kind.

BRAVE

NOT BRAVE

Plenty up top

Oman O'Malley/Cannibal Letcher | Published: JUNE 27, 2020 | Edit

I took Eileen on the Marriott's Way yesterday. It's a very scenic route through the Norfolk countryside, which used to be a railway track. The birds were singing. The weather was beautiful. The Sun was out. We were talking about history and Edward the Confessor. I was coaxed into giving her a back massage, while sat on one of those lovely little benches they have along the journey. Lord, am I pissed off that I'm not as horny as I used to be, but I still like my chicks with plenty up top!

"And get those tits in!" I said to her. "There are people who might know me, who live around here!"

"That's a big one Daddy!"

ANDREW

Do the honourable thing, and put the matter to rest...to rest, to rest, to rest.

Dea con Jack

By RUMPLESTILTSKIN | Published: JUNE 27, 2020 | Edit

I was invited into the attic of our local Vicar today, to see the stash of porn mags he'd confiscated from the choir.
"It'll take more than this to lure me back to church," I said.
I couldn't help noticing a picture of Ron Jeremy with his gift of cock in its usual receptacle. I nodded down at the scene.
"There, but for the Grace of God go you!"

I THOUGHT HARVEY WAS *A WHITE* RABBIT.

Another annoying human being joins the human race

By BIRD DUNG | Published: JULY 3, 2020 | Edit

A man was arrested today for wearing a face-mask outside a school and scaring all the children.

Sky Interviewer; "What do you think would hurt President Putin?"

By BIRD DUNG | Published: JULY 3, 2020 | Edit

Nothing you could say.

Dearest Mick,

Florence said that if I didn't get in touch with you, he would fly down here and tear every single hair I had out of my head. I hope you don't mind me writing to you after so long. A lot of water has flowed under the bridge for both of us. I'm so sorry to hear about your recent trouble. It must have been very frightening for you. As you know, Mick Florence had a similar scare not that long ago. I'm not as well as I used to be either.

Only a few evenings since, I had been talking to my lady friend, about the time we went to Malham in March and ended up sleeping in a field over-night, after the warden had caught us messing about with our brushes in the yard, and told us that we were "Not Youth Hostelling material." The miserable git banned us from ever going back.

Do you remember when we used to go to Coniston at the weekend. Can you still do those sheep impressions you had us splitting our sides with? I told my friend that you had once lifted up the side of a car, with four people in it. It may be a long time ago, but why should we forget all those precious memories.

I remember your dad very clearly. I'm very sorry to hear about your mum. She thought the world of you.

If I could live my life again there are a lot of things I would have done differently, but you can't change anything. I'm down here looking after my mum as nature intended. Do you remember Keith? He died of cancer a few years ago.

I know you are not a great letter writer, but just to let you know, I've been thinking about you.

SHOULD THIS THESPIAN HAVE STUCK TO COTTAGING?

If you don't mind hearing about how the Author gained his first sexual experiences, while cottaging cheese in the nearest public lavatory, then this is the book for you. A lot of seeds were spilt there. It proved tricky to find them again afterwards. I don't know the Author personally and did not receive any financial reward or incentive, for writing this review. There are some who think he should have stuck to acting. There is some debate about whether he actually did.

A bit cheesy by all accounts!

Reviewed by Dominic Cumberbitch *July 2020*

Taken down ^

New,

A truly tremendous read!...

If you don't mind hearing about the Author's reminiscences while cottaging cheese in the local bog. The only seeds I heard about were found balming his book-cover. I don't know the Author personally and did not receive any financial reward or incentive, for writing this review. There are those who think he should have stuck to acting. There is some debate about whether he actually did.

GUV

Unconscious bias training

By SARIN | Published: JULY 8, 2020 | Edit

Learn how to eradicate all your homophobic prejudices and become the only living zombie on the planet.

"I'm here to collect your urine sample."

Jack Sparra' maimed my marra'

By RUMPLESTILTSKIN | Published: JULY 10, 2020 | Edit

Chopped it into little pieces and smeared it on the pillow

Crushed its neck until it cried out in agony

Fed it cocaine until it blacked-out

Shat in the bed then blamed it on the cow

ZOOPHILIA

Expletive depletive

By PETER SMITH | Published: JULY 12, 2020 | Edit

Hi Rog.

Saw a post on your lass. All Annabelle's friends were making complimentary comments like;

'Isn't she lovely.'
'What a cutey!'
On the spare of the moment I wrote;
"She's just like her dad!"
Within seconds my post was taken down and I had been 'un-friended.'
You are probably right. She is 'up to something,' being so nice for a change.

APPALLINGLY RACIST BEHAVIOUR

By Blubba Blackthorn | Published: JULY 12, 2020 | Edit

Black man goes in a bar with a huge multi-coloured parrot resting on his shoulder. The bar-man stares at him in disbelief.
"Where did you get a bluddy thing like that?"
The parrot replies;
"You ought to go to Africa. Flipping millions of 'em mate!"

Little Shitzah By PETER SMITH | Published: JULY 12, 2020 | Edit

"There's a dog barking in the garden."
"It's not the only one."

DEATH SENTENCE TOO LENIENT.

HEATHER

Martin FM.   Could have sworn you told me you had no intention of ever having another relationship not that long ago and that no-one could ever match up to Rick...Had a lovely day out with Eileen on Saturday.   We cycled the Marriott's Way, and called in for a drink on our journey back. We saw four fairies in the wood and Eileen had a piss while the tractor driver fertilised the field behind her. I didn't knock it all over the table either but I did give her a hand-massage and showed her some card tricks.

I told Charles she was putting a lot of pressure on me. Mainly physical. I won't go into details.

Will have to think about your offer. The test of true love will be if his grade drops below 200. Hasn't he got huge feet...

Dear Andy

Yes, you are quite right – "No more pets. No more sweethearts. No more broken heart ..."

I did say that. And meant it. And have kept to it, for many years, up to now. So I don't know what has happened to me. I am not at all what Martin FM ought to be looking for – a nice respectable young Christian lady who still has all her bits and can make him a Daddy would be much more suitable for him, not some 90-year-old rock chick like me. As for me, the last thing I need is a man in my life ... I love being single and living alone – so it is totally silly. But totally delicious J

So far, it is all in our heads, nothing has actually happened, and we haven't even touched – apart from shaking hands at the Simul – ever. But we have a strong fascination for each other, quite apart from the chess. We've been emailing each other for over a year now, and the missives have become longer, more frequent and more affectionate, so that we have got to know each other from the inside. I went to tea, socially distanced of course, with him and his Mum – she is great and we took to each other straight away. I've been invited again J He told me we are to get married. He is a really lovely man and I hope to be able to make him happy. Is my head turned? You bet it is ...chastity is a good thing. Martin thinks it is.

He came 7th out of about 200 over the weekend in the Four Nations Chess; won the first three rounds but lost this morning and drew this afternoon. And make sure you are sitting down before you read this next bit, as I don't want your legs to give way with shock ... or make you spill your tea ...

My other cube that I ordered from China had arrived when I got home from Tona's yesterday!!! It's only taken a little over six months. I will have to give up playing my guitar and sell my kit. My hands can't cope anymore and there are no more pop concerts. At least the job retention scheme is working thanks to the Chancellor.

I'm glad you and Mrs Pumphrey had a good day out. I hope all is good between you, too.

Glad to hear you have a lock on your bed-room door at last!

**Look after yourself!
Love from Heather xxx**

Heather, I am so pleased for you. I hope you are Wells, but not for much longer, eh.

It's a match made in heaven. Martin must have had the babes beating down his door to get to him.

If I was you, I would break the news gently to Bostik first, then Keith.

He's a wonderful man (If a little odd, and eccentric, but there's me talking) and you are a wonderful woman.

There's plenty of time to get to know each other on the outside as well.

If he does break wind in bed, you will be the first to know about it.

The books he mentions probably have something to do with his missionary work in Norwich. Have you told him that you used to be a nun?

I bet his mother has been waiting for this day for a long time. I think he might like the whip.

I went down in my County game. There's no way chess can compete with a sunny garden.

214

My step-brother Kevin stole my training weights from my wardrobe while I was out on Saturday. Mum let him in.
I must warn you. I am not any good at making best-man speeches.

IT'S BEEN RAINING AGAIN. GARDEN TO DO TOMORROW. BLIND MAN COMING WEDNESDAY.

Lewis Hamilton nearly all white

By USULI TWELVES | Published: JULY 13, 2020 | Edit

And growing paler by the minute.

Up yours!

COWARDS AND SNAKES

Why not try a career in journalism, and be a "very good person"

It is all most odd Heather. I didn't feel anything, but then I did. For her suddenly to change her mind like that was so out of character, but then the pigs can be very persuasive. I made no secret of my relationship and was seen all around with her. The pigs have been spying on me for ages though, and have never really stopped harassing me since I got into trouble about twelve years ago. They have not, so far, accused me of anything. They said they were taking my phone to stop anything happening, whatever that is.   The last time they took my laptop I didn't get it back for over a year. I hadn't done anything wrong. It was just a means of keeping the pressure on. If Eileen were allowed to, she would tell you just what a kind and loving person I was to her. She was the one chasing me. What makes this worse though, is the fact, that on Thursday night before I drove her to the station we were as intimate as any couple could be. She said she couldn't wait to be with me again, and all the other things I have told you. Ruta's sister complained about me hugging her in the supermarket. I was wearing a face-mask when I did it. I have my hands full with my mum at the moment: she's started wearing her underwear over her trousers just like Superman.
I feel so tired today, but no headaches!! Thank God for the wonderful human race.

215

VULTURE, AFRICAN SAVANNA

In silent clag,
The erstwhile poet,
Peers, red-faced, at his own reflection,
And loiters,
For the Sun to rise from his back-side.

Only the *queer* folk know,
why he is such a blabber-shite.

And how to avoid,
 the sting-rays,
Emanating from his diabolical rage.

Blob Sward   Quackery Doorman
Black fly on white hair man

'Well done Mike Pence! In tonight's Vice Presidential debate you were great. Calm, composed and honest, in your defence of the President. The Interviewer handled this a lot better than the last one. Joe Biden's running mate over-ran herself, and also spoke back to you. She was unable to defend her record, because she did less than nothing to improve the situation for black minorities in the legal system. Sometimes she looked petulant,mean and arrogant (It was all in the eyes). When asked if Mr Trump would abide by the election result if it was impaired by fraudulent voting you brought up the fact that the Democrats had spent the last three years attempting to over-throw the previous election result. Along with Biden she refused to condemn the looting of shops and businesses, blaming it on inequality and unfair discrimination. Mr Trump was right to say this was not a right-wing problem! There have always been quite dramatic changes in weather, even before the influence of man. Its true to say that scientists cannot agree the degree to which mankind is responsible. Do they ever agree, about anything?'
INTERPRETED BY SKY NEWS AS A DEFINITE WIN FOR THE DEMOCRATS and post removed from Face-book.
Played down by the BBC…

NOT PLAYING BY THE RULES

By USULI TWELVES | *Published: JULY 17, 2020* | *Edit*

And they are?

Budgen's baloney

By BIRD DUNG | *Published: JANUARY 5, 2021* | *Edit*

Went into the bad supermarket for a stamp today. Libby was getting shagged round the back. One of the staff rushed up to me:
"You're banned! You know you are!"

There's only one crack worthy of the name.

Monica Evel Williams

Which one is that?

A wise-crack, of course. What did you think I meant....😦😕😜

My *niece Heather* is pregnant with a brat....I wonder if it will be born with more than one head...Lik

Stubborn old git Knighted For Walking the park

Going for a Burton.

Minister charged with rape (touching of the genitals)

By RUMPLESTILTSKIN | *Published: AUGUST 2, 2020* | *Edit*

Police chief vows; we will provide you with a much higher calibre of person in the not too distant future

Well, as fate would have it, I am looking after my dear old mum. Its my only real responsibility, apart from Sam the cat, and Primrose the rabbit of course. I've done voluntary work too, and it's a great way to broaden your mind or make new friends. When you say small dog, how small, and what breed? My favourite ones are black Spaniels because of their soft character, but I also like Jack Russell's and other varieties. 3 to 4 miles is ideal really. I cycle every day on my mountain bike. We have a track called Marriott's Way which runs past into the countryside. Its an old disused railway line. I saw a play about it on there last year under a tremendously old tree with huge branches. If I don't get out in the garden for at least a few minutes every day during this wonderful summer I get some kind of withdrawal sickness. I am very interested in history and the world around us. I'm quite a social person when I do go out, but am more at peace in quiet places or walking along a beach in summer under a half Moon. So you grew up on a council estate. Was it rough?

E HARMONY dating made simple!

Eileen B.rton...the face masks she made for us.

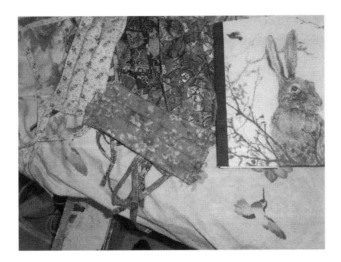

CORDELIA E. PETALWHITE

The Author was born in Surrey, in 1966, daughter of a local paint-stripper. Her father was a second-hand book seller who travelled the country selling his wares, until arrested for bigamy in 1977. She was named after an older sister, who died in childbirth. Cordelia was adopted by a local Jewish family after her mother, Clarissa, was found drugged at the bottom of a mine-shaft, and sent to boarding school at the age of twelve, where she first began writing her famous diaries. After she graduated in Economics at Cambridge she went on to become a Governess in Brussels, where she met her future husband. She eventually married Pierre White in 2004. They have three children of mixed descent and skin tone.

RACHAEL PENNINGTON BLACK

Was born in West Yorkshire but moved south to Barnsley when her father started work as a coal miner. Her original name being Penny Rimmington Black. Her early life involved having to look after her seven brothers and sisters when her father was killed in a mining accident: her mother having run off with a nearby taxidermist. She was just eleven when the house they were living in exploded, due to a faulty gas pipe. By the age of fifteen she was heavily pregnant with the first of four children. Later in life she was able to continue her education, attending the University of Paris 1922-1926, majoring in Spanish and interior design. By her mid thirties she was an accomplished pianist and had begun teaching students privately, while writing her early memoirs. Her first anthology of prose and short stories was published in 1936 to great public acclaim.

SARAH PRICE £

Idiots they may be Sarah, but haven't we all done something stupid in our lives. It is hard to believe they didn't notice something, and stop though. It seems as if the jury were convinced they did not set out to murder poor Andrew. I've never really understood this lust for punishment. The lives of the men, his wife, and the lives of their families have been turned upside down by this unfortunate incident. I believe they may have said sorry, which has to be significant. Another thing to bear in mind is that the police have often been proven to be liars. The first description I heard of this terrible accident was that Andrew had jumped on the back of their car, and had tried to hang on. Not a very wise thing to do under the circumstances, and a bit silly. I've had my bike pinched three times by people like these. I can only say, that they come from very poor backgrounds, and are probably just trying every means they can in order to survive. It would be interesting to hear some comments from serving or retired officers, if we could only coax them out of the woodwork. If Andrew had been hanging on the back I would have tried to rescue him.

We're taking the cat to be put down: bad heart, enlarged kidney, blind-as-a-bat, fur like concrete. Wish it was so easy for us...

219

FIEFDOM OF THE HORNY DOG

"We should still have a few good years ahead of us before we have to settle down at night."

"You will be able to travel on my rail staff pass"

I met Eileen a few weeks ago. We went cycling together a few times and got along very well. She rang me every night and spoke for hours. Yesterday she came across with a chocolate cake all the way from Ely. We had a great day in the garden. She knows I can't leave my mum for long. We had sex on Kittles Lane, and again outside Marsham church for a while. A man with a dog smiled from the roadside. She asked me to pull her knickers down very slowly. I've seen them down before; on Marriot's Way. Mum was on her own.

She said she loved me and that she always wanted to be by my side. Her nipples are always getting erect.

She also said the reason she left her husband for another man at work was that he was boring in bed.

Eileen had to be up early to get to work at the booking office, but still sent me lots of hugs and kisses. She said that she's been very highly aroused since they lowered her medication. She said her faith was very important.

This afternoon I received a strange message; 'I've left the gate open babes. Come straight up, but give me time to sleep. Black lingerie matters more than ever.'

When I asked her what it meant she said it was meant for Alyson. They were going on a ten-mile bike ride this afternoon.

A little later I received another message;

'I have some personal issues come up and it is no longer possible for me to continue this relationship. Please don't contact me by any means.'

She was stopped on the way home from my place a few weeks ago by the pigs, who wanted to know what she was doing here.

I know they have harassed my friend's before. Either she had another man lined up all along, or they have been round to spin their usual myths.

- **I finally realised how I buggered my back up.**

WHAT A STRANGE 24 HOURS

1 Eileen breaks up with me without giving any reason.
2 The Cops turn up and ask me for my phone.
3 Kevin comes here to gloat.

"Andrew... come and sit down to talk to Kevin..." said the Little Shitzah.

'We'll return your phone no later than Monday. If it's any later than that you can rest assured; we will be far too busy wanking over our kiddie porn.'

£When they did return the phone all the nude photos Eileen had sent of herself had been removed.

The Shitzah: "You keep treating me like a demented dwarf..." Well, you said it!

Vendor Media Group Ltd.,
The Switch,
1–7 The Grove,
Slough, SLY1 1QP,
United Kingdom.
25th July 2020

Dear Sir or madam,

I HAVE TRIED REPEATEDLY TO CANCEL MY MEMBERSHIP ON–LINE, YET YOU STILL TOOK MONEY FROM MY ACCOUNT. I NEVER ASKED FOR THIS TO BE RENEWED.
WHY DO YOU MAKE IT SO DIFFICULT TO END OUR MEMBERSHIP?
I DO NOT WANT YOU TO TAKE ANY MORE MONEY FROM MY ACCOUNT.

ALREADY UP-THE-DUFF

Good morning Benita,

Or, good afternoon. Your voice sounded very familiar? You never take a trip into Norwich??
Would you be able to do this Thursday between 3-4 pm?
You could start a jig-saw puzzle with her while you are here, and talk about doing mum's hair. I also intend buying some ceramics. On Monday we usually do the weekly shop (about 2-3).   I have had to leave her in the car for ages since the lock-down and usually find the doors have been interfered with when I get back.
If you wouldn't mind, you could sit with her in the car, or take her for a walk, while I do the shopping.
We could make these regular sessions, each Monday and Thursday of the week and you could do my shower.
Oh, I almost forgot. Before you leave each day you must provide oral-sex and finger yourself down below.

WHERE THERE'S A WILL, THERE'S A WAY...

BUTT

Here is an up-date, although I don't know why I'm even talking to you, after the way you've treated us.
Everything is alright here. I am looking after mum as well as possible. We couldn't get to your call, and then, when we rang back, AGAIN, it said the number was not a valid one. I tried to ring on my mobile too, and the same thing happened. We have tried to ring Auntie Mavis several times. I promised to keep in touch with her, so she could talk to mum, but they don't pick up the phone, and never ring back. Why don't you take your clever bolshy views and go and live in Afghanistan?
It's weird; I met the Actor Richard Burton in a dream, and was talking to him about his visit, while looking for my shoes??

I know you talked about mum coming over to Ireland, but I honestly don't think you would be able to cope. As I've said before. If you would like to give me a definite time and date, preferably in the afternoon or evening, I will make sure she is there to speak to you. WHY DO YOU REFUSE TO ANSWER AND CONTINUE TO RING WHEN WE AREN'T THERE?
I just thrashed Telemacos from Connaught 2-0 in our on-line competition. Weren't you once a chess-player yourself?

'Nothing but a dirty little slut.'

There are times when something truly unexpected happens; you suddenly realise that you love someone. You look back and remember what they were like in your arms, no matter what anyone else says to undermine your love. Sometimes we lash out when we are in shock.

There are people in this world who will do anything to destroy what they do not have, by twisting and manipulating the truth. Sometimes you just have to stand back and ask yourself why...?

Intelligent, funny and a bit crazy sometimes. Who would believe there is nearly forty years of experience between those two photographs I put up on **Just Seniors** which you looked at every day.

Donald takes out Kim with slow-acting virus
By RUMPLESTILTSKIN | Published: AUGUST 2, 2020 | Edit

It was all in the handshake, he said.

WILLIAM CLINTON
By RUMPLESTILTSKIN | Published: AUGUST 2, 2020 | Edit

'I would have taken Monica to the party, but she was a bit over-the-hill'

Comments
Kanye West declares he will run in 2020
By RUMPLESTILTSKIN | Published: AUGUST 2, 2020 | Edit

To become the first black President of the United States I presume.

HAPPY AS HELL

Bidet to ΓUN for President

Joe Biden's teeth

By SARIN | *Published: NOVEMBER 6, 2020* | *Edit*

Paid for by Ukrainian dairy farmers.

The ambulance crew

By SARIN | *Published: NOVEMBER 6, 2020* | *Edit*

Kept asking me if I'd always lived here.

EILEEN'S FLOWERS

Nancy boy

By RUMPLESTILTSKIN | *Published: NOVEMBER 12, 2020* | *Edit*
I was met outside the surgery by the same clip-board waving goon as before.Tight jeans. Hand in the
air. High-pitched voice. Spray at the ready."How can I help you today. Are you alright?"
"Why do you want to know?"
I responded with my usual curt replies and friendly demeanour.
Upon entering *Fort Knox* I made for the reception, but was told by the
receptionist I could only book over the phone for my eye appointment.
I noticed some literature laid out on a nearby table, and began to leaf
through its pages. He walked over to me.
"Why are you looking at that. What are you looking for?"
"To see if there's any gay porn!"

Early August 2020 RE; SNOWBALL

Dear Mark On-Your-collar,

It's a funny old world. I hope you don't mind me writing to you. I'm still a bit stunned, even now. When I met her, I wasn't seriously looking for anyone, but for the first time in my life I had a lady companion I could go cycling with. We had some great days, and got along very well. We talked for hours every night, until I had to remind her; she needed to get up for work in the morning. I always found her conversation a bit sexual. She said it was due to her coming off the anti-depressants. I felt as if it was all she wanted from me sometimes. It's different when you get a bit older. If only I'd met her fifteen years ago when I was in my prime. She talked a lot about settling down over here, and growing old together. I never doubted her sincerity, although I was a bit wary of the reasons she gave for leaving her husband. I'm sure there are plenty of people who are completely satisfied with 'the missionary position.' I didn't feel anything much, but then I don't sometimes, and I wasn't really very keen on going to the hotel room she wanted to book nearby for the two of us. She wanted me to go across for a meal and stay overnight, but I couldn't leave my mum for long due to her condition, so she travelled all the way over here to be with me every time she could. She seemed a bit nervous sometimes, which surprised me; but soon relaxed when I cuddled her in the chair at home. She reminded me of Little Steph, a girl I knew a long time ago. Before we met, she said how much she wanted me to hold her hand. We even cycled side by side, on Marriott's Way, with our hands held firmly together, our bikes bumping along over the ground. She put a lot of pressure on me to have sex, but I just wasn't in the mood. A lot of her conversation was very explicit. I only bought a Smart-phone so she could show me what she was doing in her bed. She said she fantasised about what it would be like when we made love.

That Thursday, we'd had a lovely day in the garden. She'd baked a chocolate cake for us. That night we were very intimate for the first time. As intimate as anyone could be really. I found her very passionate and loving. She most passionate and loving person I've known. She said she loved me and had fallen in love with me, and she hoped I would feel the same way about her one day. When I dropped her at the station, I was a bit shell-shocked after what had happened. Its ages since I was that close to anyone. She said she couldn't wait to see me again, and said she would ring me at the usual time, which she did. She sent me another message: 'I can't wait to get my mouth round your bad boy.' I will never look at Kittles Lane in quite the same way.

I was a little reluctant to commit myself fully. I decided to go with the flow. I never spoke to her much during the daytime, although she often sought my attention. It was nice to know she would always be there later though. You can grow to love someone.

On Friday morning she sent me a message to say that I was 'now *officially her man*, even when Alfie, her moggie, was around,' and that she was ending her membership on the site. I am a bit sceptical about these dating sites. You never know who you can trust, or who you are going to meet on them.

Our mutual friend sent me some messages with hearts on during the day. Then; 'I got you babe.' She said she couldn't stop thinking about me again. I misunderstood a message a bit later about leaving the gate open. It turned out to be for Alyson from work, who had wanted to go on a bike ride. A couple of hours later I received a very strange text-message, which seemed so out of character I wondered if someone else had written it. In it she said that some personal issues had come up, and she could no longer continue our relationship. She told me not to contact her by any means. I asked her what on earth had happened but never received any response.

I thought there could only be two explanations. Either she had been two-timing me all along, and it was in fact another man who had gone round to her place, *or* the Plebs had been to see her (As you may be aware, many years ago I got into trouble with a former partner. I was never malicious or threatening. I'm not that type of person). They have no right interfering in my personal relationships anyway, and god knows what rubbish they planted in her mind, if it was them. I've been getting harassed by them for years. Apparently, *you* thought I was the right one for her…

I'll understand if you don't reply Mark. She spoke a lot about you. I know you were her closest confidant. I just wanted someone to know the truth. What a way to treat the person you care about. I never did a single thing wrong to her. What a shame it should finish like this, just when we were getting to know each other. The awful thing about this is; I did feel something in the end. She said I meant 'everything to her!' Best Wishes!

"We take people completely as we find them."

"We don't like telling anyone what to do. It's all for their own good."

Go and label who you like!

For the poor prisoners of:

SAN JUAN DE LOS MORROS PRISON,
GUÁRICO 2301,
VENEZUELA,
SOUTH AMERICA.

CONTAINS TOFFEE, CHOCOLATE, PROTEIN POWDER AND WELL-MAN TABLETS

Please keep cool if at all possible

FRAGILE

HANDLE WITH CARE

Dear Mr Freeman,

As successor to the renowned Keith Simpson, I am expecting great things from you...!

1 I have been unable to get a carpenter for the house door, so it has to be left unlocked all the time.

2 I can only get an appointment at my dentist in a year and a half's time.

3 My friend had to wait three hours for an ambulance when she had fallen and broken her ankle in three places.

4 I am still getting harassed by the Cops, after contacting an ex-partner on the phone eleven years ago.

$ *Biden sure does love that face-mask. It takes years off him.*

Sudesh Amman 'lawful killing'

By USULI TWELVES | Published: AUGUST 20, 2021 | *Edit*

Hostel staff unable to search his room for knife due to "lack of training."

225

St. Michael's Presbytery,
Gresham Queer-Copse,
Parson's Privilege,
Little Tots Lane,
CANTERBURY.

Dear Archbishop,

I attended the public execution of Herbert Prophet, the common leech-collector, convicted of rope-smuggling in Bristol, last month. It was a very enjoyable affair, with a huge audience of both Catholics and First Day Adventists. We tucked into our ham sandwiches and quaffed our half of bitter. When someone whispered that he might actually be innocent, we all burst out laughing, and pretended to be strangled.

Damned is his soul for all creation!

*With regards to your compulsion to want to masturbate outside a school. I would advise you to wait until home time.

Yours politely,
Senior Rev George P. McVicar,
Ineverfukdmyhousekeeper.

Kidnapping of 300 Nigerians schoolgirls

By ADUMLA | Published: FEBRUARY 27, 2021 | Edit

At least none of them will have to worry about dying a virgin!

(I hear Rolf Harris has been spotted peering in an empty window). Rich is the land of Opportunity!

ENTRAPMENT: Pigs posing as pupils fully-supported by Parliament ✓

'It's 1996. I'm on a Men's Development course at Leeds Road Hospital. All the top managers are here. There are some nice blokes. I'm surprised by one or two. We are here to learn about empathy, and listening to others. Martin sits at the head of the circle with a local Writer; a humanist and poet. They are inviting one of us to come to the front and share our life story. It can be as harrowing as we like, as long as we are honest. If I do, there'll be no turning back...'

I'm beginning to think the President is making too many silly misjudgements. What's wrong with keeping a dignified silence, until all the votes are in!!!? Ginger Vitus Curse the god who made me.

How is checking that the votes are not all from Hilary Clinton an attack on democracy?

We have a new Carer called Donna here to look after the beast. Nice legs and tits. Time will only tell if she has been sent from the Sycamore group to spy on us.

Red devil given suspended sentence; pigs refused the bribe

By GODFREY WINKLEBACKER | Published: AUGUST 26, 2020 | Edit

Well, it worked before!

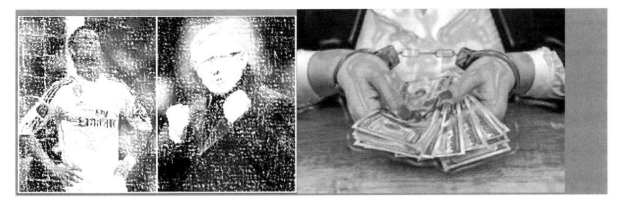

Pupil power forces Government U-turn

A "VICTORY FOR COMMON SENSE"

Nice arse, by the way..."FACE MASKS SCARING THE CHILDREN" – claims head teacher.

Sharp rise in corona virus cases on campus
too busy bonking to think about social distancing.

OUT OF FUEL

Like a jet engine,
Fired from an imaginary gun,
Towards the horizon,
In this 65th year,
I gave up trying.

Slowly grinding to a halt,
On this bumpy lane,
In the flowers of the night,
With Marie crying.

The hail of winter,
Over my head,
Crashing down upon the asphalt.

So many journeys I have made,
Upon this speckled land.

If you, my love, could know,
Wherein the hot regions of the snow,
The machine of my youth abandoned,
And death became its shadow,
In this world of make-believe.

Wrong sis?

By GODFREY WINKLEBACKER | Published: JANUARY 7, 2021 | Edit

And a Happy New Year to you too!

You make me smile.

haha!

What's matter. Can't you sleep?

Not so far.

I have an idea I can help.

?

Think of something very large.

Like What?

Think of something very hard.

What is it?

It's cold outside. Why don't you try sucking on your fingers to start with.

WTF You made me feel very uncomfortable. I am eighteen, and in a relationship.

Sorry!

Those were *repugnant* messages you sent last night. Please do not go near her in the supermarket.

Had to stand guard, while Eileen had a piss

I had to stand guard, while Eileen had a p..,
On that cycle track, which everyone knew,
Travelling up from the city.

Her knickers at half mast,
Holding up her dress,
In case anyone saw her,
And fainted.

Dear Fosters (November 2020),

I applied for a DBS check as Simon kindly suggested. It cost me £90, not ten pounds, and was a complete waste of time and money. I have been trying to get it done for the past three weeks causing me even more stress and anxiety. It was completely lacking in detail and dates. I told the DBS you could never trust the police anyway. The last thing I want is to ask them for anything.

As I said, the police have threatened to smash down my door on more than one occasion. Who is doing anything to challenge these idiots? It would be a complete waste of time writing to the Police Commissioner, the Home Secretary, the IPCC or my MP. I have tried these routes before.

I wanted to know:

1 Which Court awarded the order (I thought it was Norwich Magistrates, but they say they have no record).

2 I wanted to know what sexual offence I was put on the Register for.

(I think Simon made a little joke about this. It is actually a more intriguing question than you may think).

3 I wanted to know when the order was granted (I think it was around July/August 2010).

I didn't receive a reply to my original letter, which I presume has something to do with my label or the fact I have not paid you anything so far. Simon did hint it could cost thousands of pounds to get this information using a Solicitor.

Is there anyone on this planet who gives a damn, or who doesn't have the Corona-virus as an excuse for complete indifference?

Nearly twelve years ago I contacted a former partner I didn't even want when we slept in the same bed, on the telephone. There was one land-line call, and one disputed text message (which, quite frankly, could have come from anyone). Nothing I said was either malicious or threatening. At the close of my sentence the police applied for a Court order with the Magistrates. I was not on any order and was not the dangerous person they insisted I was. They brought up an unfortunate incident on a train, which had happened more than thirty years ago.

A few weeks ago, they suddenly turned up at my home demanding to have my mobile phone. My then girlfriend (Aged 61) had inexplicably finished with me. I still do not know why. When they returned my phone, after looking through all my personal messages, I noticed that all the saucy pictures she had sent me had been removed. I know. They have a 'very difficult job...' *counting all their doe!*

It was some relief this August to feel I was no longer on the order. It had been granted in 2010 for ten years. This September morning the police again turned up at my home. I'd had a poor night. I suffer from debilitating headaches and fatigue. I can't walk very far due to bad arthritis in both my knees. I was extremely shocked to see them and I told them why. These raids have been going on for the last ten years. One of them spotted a kitchen knife lying in the garden, which I had left on a bin cover by mistake. They told me that my order was not in fact finished, and that the starting date for the order was one year after it was granted. They told me that if I did not interact with them in a positive way they would apply for a warrant and send a dozen officers round straight away to break down the door. They said they would also log it as a 'refusal,' and take me back to court again.

I am currently looking after my mum, who is becoming increasingly fragile. She is always very upset by these visits. I have written to my own MP countless times in the past, but it has been an absolute waste of time. Solicitors are expensive and often collude with the Authorities.

Causes of suspicion:

- o We have a Carer who assists me with the care of my mother. I have been seen in town with her. She's 21 but looks a lot younger.
- o I regularly cycle along a nearby footpath, where I bumped into some of these con artists.
- o I have a new girlfriend, who's picture you can see on my page.

I know for sure that they look at everything I write, because some of the local church pork-chops reported it to them and wanted them to arrest me.

$ **"We don't like to have anyone on the Register."**

"In that case why do you try so bluddy hard to get them on it??"

Brain-dead chicken-headed pea-brained pieces of mutton-shit.

Dear Fosters (Simon),

I spoke to you briefly on the phone a few weeks ago. I hope you don't mind me contacting you again concerning the matters we spoke about.

I had hoped to live my life in peace and not to have to bother with all this. It causes me unbelievable stress. I also have an elderly mother to look after.

I would really appreciate if you could read what I have to say closely.

<u>THE FACTS</u>

1 Nearly twelve years ago I pleaded guilty to contacting my ex-partner on the phone. There was one land-line call in which I clearly said that I was sorry about a misunderstanding, and one disputed text message. I broke a restraining order not to contact her. Admittedly, the circumstances were rather fraught.

2 The policeman who answered my call had been carrying on a relationship with my ex. He put on a funny voice pretending to be her. He said in his statement that I shouted and swore down the phone, which was not true and stood there grinning at me in the Courtroom.

3 Nothing I did was either malicious or threatening, although I did act rather rashly, and foolishly.

4 Nothing was ever said about the property belonging to me which my ex still had at the house.

5 Around August 2010 the police applied for a SOPO order, claiming I was in danger of committing a serious sexual offence such as rape, against my ex-partner, or a member of the public, before the Magistrates in Norwich. When I said this was absolute rubbish I was ordered to shut up or I would be taken down.

(My ex-partner is someone I didn't even want when we slept in the same bedroom. I wouldn't have touched her for a million pounds).

*The order said I was not to contact or conduct a search on my ex-partner or either of her children or go back to the area, and to leave my computer open to scrutiny. I think that's all that's on it. I have not broken it. The fact that her children were placed on the order makes me sound like some kind of paedophile. I treated them both with complete propriety and kindness the whole time I knew them. I was never charged with any kind of sexual offence against them or any other children.

6 I was not on the Sex-offenders Register when the police applied for the SOPO, but as a result of them getting the order they were able to put me on it for ten years, as I understand it.

7 Throughout the ten years, I have suffered continuous harassment: raids on my home, malicious stories put all around town and with neighbours, followed wherever I go, interference in my mail and everything I do. What I've been through has utterly ruined my health. I cannot sleep at night because of anxiety, headaches and bad nightmares.

8 In 2011 I did think about leaving the area where it was impossible to live, and travelled over to Ireland to be near my relatives, but they were waiting for me there, to cause trouble, so I came home. I did not break the law by doing this, and apparently came back in time.

9 In about May, I think, of the following year, they took me back to Court, for not telling them I had some writing published under a pseudonym, and for not declaring that I had used my step-father's surname when applying for an e-mail address. I was fined about £500, but they were not able to put me on probation, which is what they were seeking.

10 I was relieved when it got to August this year, because that's when I should have come off the Register (I should not have been on it in the first place, in my opinion. It was just a way of keeping tabs on me).

Back they came again! They said I must start to have a more positive attitude towards them, or else...

I had been having a relationship with a grown woman close to my own age (I'm nearly 65). We had just become intimate and she said she loved me. Then she sent me a most odd message, saying that some personal issues had come up and I was not to contact her by any means. The following morning the police came for my phone, bursting into my bedroom on a Saturday morning. There was nothing illegal on it of course, but when they did return it, the saucy pictures, she had sent me, had been removed.

They told me that they had to intervene "to stop something bad from happening." I have no idea what they mean.

11 In September of this year, they returned yet again, and told me that if I didn't interact with them in a positive way, they would record it as a 'refusal,' return with a search warrant and smash down the door, and take me back to Court again.

I said I was surprised to see them again because I didn't think I was on the Register any more.

They told me that the start date for the ten-year period began one year after it was granted.

When is someone going to do something? There must be someone around with the back bone to stand up to these bullies. I'm willing to answer any questions you have. I realise that representing someone with such a label is extremely daunting and anathema in the legal profession, which is why they are able to get away with so much. I do however, look forward to hearing from you, as this letter should perhaps constitute an initial consultation.

Yours Sincerely,

BUNDERCHOOK

P S Could the police be made to pay for your fees, if they are proved to have lied? I'll understand if you are unable to take my case or get involved. LABELS. I'd rather you didn't discuss this letter with the Plebs.

Foster's REPLY: <u>You can always spend a few thousand *trying* to find out, if the Court don't have any record or try the DBS. It'll cost about £10 (£90).</u>

<u>Reply from the DBS: Your request for information regarding the date of the order, the Court granting the order, and the reason the order was granted has not been provided by our magnificent friends down on Gravel Row. *A complete waste of time and money then?* **NO REPLY.**</u>

Dear Mss Saunders,

As a matter of great urgency, could you please advise Chloe Smith about the contents of my message, as this involves the tampering of mail by the police. I include here, my original letter, with one or two minor grammatical corrections. I can only surmise why you did not receive it. I am truly sorry to have to write to her, or anyone else, about all

this. It's as distressing to me, as it must be to those reading my letter. I do see how this would be a difficult issue for her to deal with, let alone answer. As I said in my e-mail, I really just wanted to know if she had 'received,' my letter, as I have suspected for some time that my mail was being interfered with.
I feel like a bit of a nuisance, with so much going on at the moment.

Dear Chloe Smith,

I had thought of writing to the Head of Norfolk Constabulary, until I saw who it was. I try not to judge a book by its cover, but in this case its probably best to do just that. Another option would have been the Police and Crime Commissioner, but can they be trusted? Who are they? From what I have read they are still fully paid-up Members of the Establishment, and keep very well in with the police (The IPCC are anything but independent, and have been shown for what they are a number of times. Everyone knows they are weak and ineffective at standing up to the force). How on earth can I write to someone with a name like 'Jerome Mayhew?'
I wrote to the Home Secretary a number of years ago about police harassment, but did not receive a reply.
My problem concerns the past. A long time ago I got into trouble. All I want now is a quiet life. I spend most of my time studying or looking after my mum. I have not been in the best of health in recent years and some days I can hardly walk. It feels as if there is no-one who even gives a damn. I cannot afford to spend thousands of pounds on a Solicitor who cannot even be bothered to listen. Surely the virus can't be blamed for everything...

About twelve years ago I contacted an ex-partner on the phone. There was one land-line call in which I wanted to clear up a silly misunderstanding, and one disputed text message, which could have been sent by anyone. I was never at any moment malicious, nasty or threatening. I know for certain I did not shout or swear on the phone as the officer who had been having a relationship with my ex, and who was in her house, claimed. My relationship with my ex had broken down because I did not want to touch her. I had been depressed for some time about a lot of things. While I was with her, I pleaded guilty to one offence of 'exposure,' where a shop assistant passing some trousers through a changing room curtain saw that I was naked from the waist down, for two to three seconds. There was no sexual activity. It was classed as simple 'exposure,' yet I was placed on the Sex-offender's Register for it.

When I contacted my ex on the phone, I broke a restraining order not to contact her. No mention was made of my property which was still around the house. Because I was on this Register, I ended up receiving two and a half years in prison. A lot of things have been said about me which are simply not true.

Near the end of my sentence the police applied for a SOPO order, and had the cheek to name my ex's two children on the order. I was nothing but kind and loving to both of them. They claimed that upon my release I was in danger of raping my ex-partner or a member of the community. When I stood up and said this was absolute rubbish, I was threatened with incarceration by the Magistrates. As a result of them getting the order they were allowed to put me on the Sex-offenders Register for a whole ten years! I was not on it at that point. Since leaving prison I have been the subject of continuous harassment and prejudice, not only by the PPU (Who in their own words are a 'law unto themselves.') I have found it hard to settle down, but I have eventually managed to make something of my life. I did try to start a small writing group and joined a chess club, but the police were always going around telling everyone about me and spoiling everything. Whenever I go out there's always a police car following me around, or a helicopter circling over-head. The Authorities must have money to burn to waste all their hard-earned resources on me. I'm beginning to think we are being watched here, or they have placed a camera somewhere in the back garden. There was a time when I would have done anything to help the police. I was never brought up to break the law. One of my best friends in town is a retired police woman. My sister has done everything she can to get me out on the streets, even before her marriage began to turn sour.

When it got to August this year, I breathed a sigh of relief. The original order had been granted sometime around July/August 2010. I had recently started a relationship with a lady from Ely, who, at 61, was just a bit younger than myself. We had just become intimate. She said she loved me and had visited my home several times. The next day she continued to send me wonderful messages. Then she sent me one which was so odd I wasn't even sure if it was from her. She said that some personal issues had come up and I was not to try and contact her by any means. The next morning the police burst into my home while I was in bed, demanding to have my mobile phone. When they did eventually return my phone, the saucy pictures she had sent me had been removed. They said they would continue to harass me for the rest of my life. I am sure they are having a good laugh when they get back to their car. About three weeks later the police returned again. They said that unless I interacted positively with them, they would record it as a 'refusal,' and take me back to court again. They also threatened to return with several officers to batter my front door down if need be.

CAN YOU SEE NOW WHY NO-ONE LIKES THE POLICE, OR IS NO-BODY IN PARLIAMENT REALLY BOTHERED?

I said that I was surprised to see them, because I was no longer on the Register.

THEY TOLD ME THAT MY INCLUSION ON THE REGISTER ONLY BEGAN A YEAR AFTER IT WAS GRANTED, AND THAT I WOULD HAVE TO SPEND ANOTHER YEAR ON THE REGISTER BEFORE I COULD BE FREE OF THEM.

I have read of the police taking all sorts of appalling liberties with anyone they don't like.

THE POLITICIANS WILL NOT LIFT A LITTLE FINGER TO DO ANYTHING ABOUT IT!

The Court had no record of me so I tried to find out the truth through the DBS but ended up spending £88, plus a lot of phone calls, for absolutely nothing. The police would not tell them:
1 The Court where the order was granted.
2 The date.
3 What sexual offence I was placed on the order for.
4 When it would expire.
I'm not sure if your reputation will be able to survive any kind of communication with such a terrible individual like me, so I will understand if you are unable to respond in any way. I have spoken to you on the phone a very long time ago when I lived elsewhere and found you a very nice person.

I did write to you about eight years ago on a similar theme but you couldn't get involved as I no longer lived in your area. I could risk trying to contact the Home Secretary again...but I think she will be too busy. If she's in a bad mood I might even get a clip round the ear. Passing my letter to Mr. Mayhew may have stirred up a hornets' nest, as he will surely contact the Head of Constabulary. I've just been banned from Face-book for posting a picture of Adolf Hitler...!

Trump supporters shot, trying to defend Democracy

By GODFREY WINKLEBACKER | Published: JANUARY 7, 2021 | Edit

Do you trust the Democrats?

A very *cavalier* attitude SHUT-UP!

COUNSELLOR

Why the awkward silences,
As you sit with your book,
Inverting your pencil over the manual,
Avoiding my gaze,
Occasionally smiling, into the distance.

You, who like to be honest,
When the chips are down,
Your self-preservation,
With the Over-lord's threat.

Undermining your leader's resolve,
In the special needs room,
Where your tropical plants thrived.

Even though, kind,
Do you still have a heart,
For those who you pushed,
Over the edge...?

'A flying turkey with wings of ivory, from the farthest reaches of the galaxy, destined to become tomorrow's quintessential pariah. Short stories, anecdotes and acuity, enough to split your sides. Contains information far too rude for adolescents or your private physician. Brings together a train-load of vital evidence about why mankind is such a smart-arse, but missing a Satnav with directions on how to get your end away. An ether-dragging voyage through the corridors of time, spanning the years before the first nuclear missiles landed in Kim Jong-un's back passage. 'Wrong on so many levels,' claim Scottish clergy. 'Water off a duck's back.' replies the Author. A volume of work considered by many experts to warp the very extremities of space in an age where black lingerie matters more than ever.' STARMASTE

Brave Melania gives hope a boost

By GODFREY WINKLEBACKER | Published: AUGUST 26, 2020 | Edit

How proud he must have been...! *He didn't seem himself in the debate on Tuesday night?*

THE PRESIDENT

By PETER SMITH | Published: NOVEMBER 8, 2020 | Edit

Mr President. The best way to deal with this is by showing magnanimity and generosity towards the apparent Victor. Apologise for the jokes you made about him and give him credit where it is due, even though the use of postal ballots is very much open to scrutiny. Be compassionate in your understanding of his uphill struggles in life. This will demonstrate that you are actually the better man. By holding out the hand of friendship to Joe Biden you will help to heal the country and set a great example to everyone. History will be kinder to you than you know.

Not unless you can get a clear shot at him, to wipe the gleam off his tusks. *I heard they found some ballot boxes on the Moon.*

Poachers Pocket   September 2020

Went for a meal with Mila on Saturday. She's a mother of 4 from the Philippines, who has small hands, and, according to Heather, looks like a beauty queen. She thinks we make a handsome couple. I predict that one day Mila will lie back on my bed, groaning in ecstasy, while I drink from the hairless cup..I'd like to get to know her gradually. She said likewise.

As she was getting out of the car I remarked: "that's one helluva chest!"

"You're not the only one to say that," she smiled. Mila should have been called Mona. She's a generation younger than me. Oh, shucks! Something I will have to learn to live with I guess (That's two in as many months. Wonder if I should go for a hat-trick?).

- On Friday I got to know her a lot better on King Street under the street lamp.
- Her nipples will be thick and dark like pure sepia. How about that for a fantasy, you ignorant cretins!
- Then Mila said: "There's plenty more, if you want it!"

Egyptian oil lamp

The Egyptian oil lamp,
In my bedroom,
Is filled with snakes and
Dancing girls.

Honey seeps from its light,
And stars escape with the dawn.

Once more, unto the breach dear friends. Can't stay, blue-jay!

Normal on the phone *By GODFREY WINKLEBACKER / Published: MARCH 1, 2021 / Edit*

Shite-in-the-butt was normal on the phone when she rang during mum's birthday party...

"I don't want to hear a single word 'that' repugnant creature moaning in the background has to say..."

"Keep taking the tablets...!"

Do you mean the ones you were on?

From the office of Mr. Mayhew: *'We do not want to hear from you again. The Head of Constabulary has got better things to do with his time!'*

ON BENEFITS

By <u>HERPES ZOSTER</u> | *Published: JANUARY 22, 2021* | <u>*Edit*</u>

HIM

Dollops of doe in the pocket

2nd hand camper van in the car-park

Never speaks

Never smiles

Several sprogs to various girls around the city

No work, due to the pandemic

Huge family rodent

Lots of mates calling round

Delivers a dozen large blue plastic containers full of clothes to the poor of Trinidad and Tobago each year

Doesn't really live there

HER

Never finishes a job

Always dressed in fine clothes

Free new house to live in

Always giggling

Wears the outfits of a ten-year-old

Always on her smart-phone

Bullmastiff pup with enough tits to feed an army

Always wants more

First pregnancy

Always late or absent

Glazed eyes on a Thursday

Little brothers never caught COVID-19 from the kids at school

Dear Tom, and Mr. Mayhew,

You would be in agreement that e-mails between us should remain confidential though?
As I said before. Anything which calls itself 'independent,' probably isn't.
I didn't want to approach the police directly, for obvious reasons.
If you recall, I simply wanted to know:
A What offence I had committed to be placed on the Register, and when?
B Why the police had added an extra year for no apparent reason?
C What Court granted the order, and when it should have expired?
D Why they were continuing to threaten me (and possibly why they were interfering in my relationships;
    these people went all round town telling people the most stupid nonsense about me)?
It doesn't take a month of Sundays to answer such simple questions.
The Tory party does have a reputation for sucking up to the police somewhat.
All I really want is for someone to tell the truth, and to be able to get on with my life.

Chaos in America

By <u>RUMPLESTILTSKIN</u> | *Published: JANUARY 9, 2021* | <u>*Edit*</u>

The Democrat pack are finally going to have another go at impeachment, having tried to get Donald Trump out of office any way they could, over the last four gruelling years. They are hoping to rush it through before the end of his tenure. The TV debates exposed some of Trumps weaknesses, but he also has many admirable qualities too: he isn't afraid to stand up to the Establishment. Twitter have bowed to pressure and removed his account, but how often does that happen for the silliest and pettiest of reasons. So much for free-speech. Trump has always discouraged violence and law-breaking. Is it only me who can see what a bitch Pelosi is? Bidet called the demonstrators a mob, who did not represent America. There are another seventy million voters who are also very angry. It's likely that the Democrats did pull a fast one. It wasn't long ago that Trump was being criticized for just the same kind of language. How are you supposed to react when you feel you are being robbed?

Dear Mr Mayhew (January 2021),

I don't know who else to talk to about this. I'm tired out looking after a sick mother who sometimes takes my post and I'm not very well myself. Apparently, I have been caught breaking the 30-mph speed limit driving through Roughton, two months ago. I recall someone pointing a hand-held speed gun at me on my weekly route to the supermarket, standing beside a cop-car, sometime around then…

1 I have been threatened with a £1000 fine and the loss of my licence.
2 The letter I received did not tell me what documents I had to send.
3 I have been totally unable to get through to anyone at the police station.

What on earth is going on in this rotten country. If something isn't done about it soon, I can see there being serious rioting on the streets.

The squealers have started trying to take my writing down again, since I wrote to you. Does anyone even give a damn?

VIRUS FIGHTS BACK

By SARIN | Published: JANUARY 22, 2021 | Edit

Billions spent on vaccines blinking useless against new strains.

Dear Mr. Mayhew,

I've just heard: the lily-livered Bailey has decided to jump ship rather than answer the questions I raised. To be honest, there's not much to choose from any of these longtails.

A staunch defence of the church

I'm happy with Donna's care of my mum.
We have a game of dominoes after the jobs are done.
'There are quite a lot of teachers at the Community church,' I said.
"They love controlling everyone. Some of the congregation can hardly read or write.
There are others who look as if they have just escaped from the mad house."
Her husband had three kids with her, and 3 with his ex-wife. She was 15. He was 30.
"So, are you a friend of that Grimsey woman?" I asked. "She's very influential in town."
Donna glanced down at my pants.
"There's nowt s queer as folk," she grimaced, half-smiling, half-laughing...

Donna swore that she had never used any bad-language in her life.

Dear Tom and Jerry, Seriously, how do you expect me to get evidence of police interference when they are able to manipulate the system so effectively and are often encouraged to do so by the Government. I wouldn't imagine the IOPC would do anything more than go through the motions.
My 'evidence' could be said to be circumstantial (unless you can think of another word). I have noticed particular files disappearing for instance, and their knowledge of my dating site activity always seems to be very specific. I am allowed to use dating sites by the way, unless they can think of a reason why I shouldn't. They could always invent another reason why I shouldn't. The police have so many resources and power at their disposal that a mere citizen doesn't stand a chance. I fully support the lock-down, but interrogating a man for smoking in his car, is just another reason why we have to question this authority. I hope that in the original letter to them you were able to ask the questions which I related to you. I am very poorly at the moment with fatigue and prolonged headaches. I very much appreciate your time and patience. The Met have had months to answer your letter. Is this how the Tory party deals with bullies?

NEW VACCINE SHRINKS YOUR COCK

By BIRD DUNG | Published: JANUARY 26, 2021 | Edit

There is absolutely no evidence that it does, but how can you afford to take any chances...Effectiveness of first injection down to 0.1%. A man in Scotland grew a new pair of ears. The next day his leg fell off!

Let it be known, that the increasing cases of the new strain are caused by idiots not having the vaccine, and not by air-passengers from India and Pakistan spreading it all over the fking streets of Lancashire.
MATHEW HANDCOCK

Dear Norfolk Constabulary Shit-heads,

I have been unable to speak to anyone on the phone. I have tried several times. No-one has ever responded to my e-mails in the past. I wrote to you yesterday. About seven months ago I was caught speeding through Roughton. It's the bit where the speed limit suddenly changes from 40 to 30 mph. I was doing 42. I paid my fine as soon as I knew. I thought that was the end of it. Now I find that the offer of a fine has been withdrawn because I didn't send my driving licence in. I still don't know where to send it. I am not trying to avoid getting my licence endorsed. I have a sick mother to look after, and being dragged into Court will only cause a lot more stress and anxiety.

Dear Mr. Mayhew, and Tom,

I've had a little think about this speeding fine. I really want to be totally honest.

I do seem to remember something about sending my driving licence in, having paid the fine.

At that time the post was very unreliable. We hadn't had any deliveries for ages.

I was very worried about sending my licence in the post, because I thought it might get lost or stolen. A lot of Post Office staff seemed to be away sick. There are many sick people at the Post Office. I think I must have held back, but then forgot about it. This is fairly typical of me.

They never got in touch with me, even though they had my details.

Methinks I must protest

By GODFREY WINKLEBACKER | *Published: MAY 16, 2021* | *Edit*
Hi Janet, I understand what you mean about letting mum move the furniture around all day and night. It doesn't hurt anyone, although it can get a bit exasperating. She often leaves things all over the floor which she could trip-up on, and she sometimes spills things which leave a sticky mess.

My mum always liked to play tricks on us all. She is human!

Mr. Trump.

Surely, it's a bit shallow judging someone at first glance on their hair-style.

I don't know where your 'fiddler' is but I'm sure it will turn up soon on the side of her leg. It was kind of you to bring it round, but I guess you will ignore me when you see me on the street now…

PATHOGRAPHY

Emerged into a region of Northern Europe notorious for its drinking and brawling to parents who were constantly bickering, during the time of the Suez crisis. Mother still claimed to be a virgin, even during child-birth. Father a semi-literate womanizer and practical joker whose favourite pastime was picking out his ear with a matchstick stalk or pointing his shot-gun at the crows. At the age of four the Author was sent to be brain-washed at the nearby Catholic primary school. Impotent from the age of sixteen, he was taught a lesson by his sister's boyfriend, after a pair of her knickers went missing from the junkyard. A stint at the Boy's Grammar school resulted in a serious case of sleeping-sickness. He received six of the best for setting fire to the Headmaster's study because O'Melia put the blame on him. For years the Author continued to endure considerable physical and mental abuse from both his parents. Dad left home after a row about greasy chips and stains on the carpet. He trained as a football referee, but never took part in any matches. Art college soon followed, as did alopecia, but not before he was arrested for vagrancy, while working as a road-sweeper and an emptier-of-shit-buckets. Suffering from an over cautious and highly-strung disposition the Author gained a reputation for being slightly odd and eccentric. He was considered far too mad by his contemporaries. Andy entered a railway Signal-box at the age of twenty-five, continuing his studies where he left off, occasionally punching holes in the wall and putting the finishing touches to some much-needed cosmetic surgery. The Author terrified a group of young carol singers who had called at his home by partly exposing himself to them during a rendition of 'Away in a manger'. While working as a train conductor-guard in the south of the country, with free travel wherever he pleased, the author was arrested yet again for getting his manhood out in public. After working as an Instructor in Occupational therapy for five years, in charge of education resource and Art therapy, the author lost his job for non-disclosure on his application form. More care work followed, looking after a Catholic priest, for the Society of Marius, in Walsingham. In 2007 he was imprisoned for having a museum fire-arm without a licence, discovered at his holiday home by a gang of marauding cob-rollers. Following his release onto the Norfolk broads the Author was repeatedly harassed and made homeless. A long-term relationship ended in disaster when a neighbour reported seeing him peering over her fence. His Writer's circle was constantly being interrupted by pigs barging in through the side doors. Neighbours accused the Author of being a *Peeping Tom* after a series of letterboxes were discovered to have fingerprints on them in the mornings.

A number of vehicles which had been damaged in the Resident's car-park and a stolen motor-cycle were also similarly attributed to the pariah.

In November 2018 the Author began to study chess and at the same time discovered he had the innate ability to change shape. It wasn't long before he was being asked to play for the County team. For three years the Author had been suffering from early Cecil Parkinson's and was becoming doubly incontinent. He continues to be a well-known bogey-man on the lanes of the county, steaming along on his black Cannondale mountain bike, and causing a stench wherever he rides.

B A (Hons) Fine Art
Astrological Consultant D.M.S. (Astrol.)
Teacher of Paget-Gorman signed speech
Former arm-wrestler and Country show-man
Interpreter of dreams
Able to track down any living creature across the known Universe
SOCIAL COMMENTATOR OF WORLD RENOWN
Expert in Counter Intelligence and the gathering of information
Winner of the Koestler award for literature.
Contender for the *Prix Goncourt*.
Major novel (1996)

Short story writer and poet. Political satirist.
Winner of the Welsh Open poetry competition.

Other books by the same Author:
BUNDERCHOOK STARWORD POET(Revival). Widening Underground, Criminal Tendencies, Offensive Behaviour, Alien Intelligence, Odd bent Coppers, Natural Surveillance, Trades of the Toadman, **Dance of the red-crowned Prince, Thunderbuck Ram Art-work, Philistines, Angels and Queries. King Simon's yellow bull-frog, BLUNDERBUSS-S STARBOARD PARROT. Inappropriate contact/content, Yoda's drum. Blunderbuck Starbird Pirate: Retarded Development.** *Curse of the Wallingford Stalker.*

Brighter than the day

By GODFREY WINKLEBACKER | Published: JANUARY 27, 2021 | Edit

There is a time, when we must rise,
From darkness, pain and wrath,
When we are stumbling on our knees,
And black is but the cloth.

When children pray,
And old men say,
That life is just too bad…

Should I eclipse the Sun and Moon,
The stars by which we live,
Should I be fain to shine the way,
From fear and loss of life.

There is a light from this foul world,
Which guides us from the void,
An angel which was sent by God,
To bring us to his side.

Tightening of the claws

From the tea-stained ground,
Where you dragged your bad leg,
I lifted you up to my chest,
And held you close,
Feeling the life within you.

Your blank eyes filled with a distant alarm,
No longer able to see the world,
In that grey garden, where you roamed, after midnight.

For one second longer,
The soft fur hollow, lingered on the chair,
For your last ride,
Into the city,
And your pink-padded embrace,
Gently tightened its grip,
Around my fingers.

Little brown owl

Soft little owl,
Made from scraps of felt,
And sewn together,
With brown thread, long ago,
Perched in my palm forever.

Pushed into my pocket,
On our paper round,
By one more precious than the rain.
The End (or almost!)

239

Stone-Wall Jackson

In the distant mist,
The blonde-bean-pole,
Whispered to Martin.
Mustering his troops into battle.

I erupted, like a deranged bull,
Spewing out smoke from my nostrils,
A picture of Martha on my mind,
And that head-lock,
Where, he'd forced my surrender.

From just beyond our penalty area,
I rumbled down-hill.
Past the centre-circle,
sucking up soil,
With my sole-studs.

Daley groaned there in the mud,
Blood pouring from both his ears,
His back-broken and his hand,
Held up to the Sun like a shield.

I ploughed on,
With 'Jacko' wringing his leather gloves,
And that clever-dick smile of his,
In the goal-mouth.

Like an impending juggernaut,
I gathered speed,
My legs churning like pistons,
Bouncing over the runnels,
While he watched our Captain,
Dribbling the ball,
To the corner flag.

The droplet burst like a cough of flame,
And hovered in the air above them,
As Jacko rose,
Near the goal-post.

I braced my shoulder for full impact;
And hit him with the accumulated power,
Of a million neutron bombs,
Right bang, smack in his chest,
Just as he was turning to catch the ball…
Haha!

Spinning on the hard turf,
With muck all over my rear-end,
I wondered what frigging day it was,
Wheezing like an old hen.

Trying to catch my breath,
Gushing with each hollow rasp of my lung,
As he booted the ball,
Far up field.

Hi Leo,

Felt I had to answer what you said a little more thoroughly. I was brought up to protect women. I disliked anyone who was rough or violent. My moral up-bringing convinced me that women were the gentler sex and that they needed our protection. There are situations where this is still true. I thought it was wrong to take advantage of a woman, under any circumstances, unless your name is Leo of course!

However. We find ourselves in an age where women are seeking to dominate men in their quest for power. Men (at least some men: mainly white Anglo-Saxon men) are often seen as the enemy. Men seem to be taking the blame for everything.

There are occasions when women think they have been forced to have sex against their will, yet sex itself can be quite an aggressive act. This is not the fault of men, but simply nature.

How many times have women lied in the newspapers, just to get men into trouble?

To be sorry for hurting someone seems on the face of it, to be very commendable, yet, remorse of conscience is itself 'indecent.' To leave our actions of yesterday in the lurch, when we acted with the very best of intentions, based on who we were then, on the information we had available to us, then.

I leave you with something Nietzsche said about women:

'The complete woman perpetrates literature; in the same way she does a little sin. As an experiment, in passing, looking round to see if anyone notices, so that someone notices.'

I hope some of this makes sense at six o'clock in the morning.

SUDDEN IMPACT

She boarded the night train to Penzance, and waved goodbye to her mother. It was raining but the evening sunshine splashed light all over the window. This journey would change the rest of her life, forever.

Katy was looking forward to the visit. She opened her book and began reading. After a while she dozed off, but woke to eat some of her sandwiches.

There was no Moon tonight, but the compartment was bright and comfortable. Time passed quickly as the train stopped at several stations on the way.

It must have been about half seven, when she saw a shadow in the corridor. A man looked in and began fiddling with the latch. He came in and slid the door back behind him.

He sat down opposite, placing a ruck-sack on the seat. Then he began reading from a book about traffic accidents.

"This is the train to Penzance?" he asked.

She nodded, and buried her head back inside the pages of her novel.

The man continued to make polite conversation, but then he began to rummage in his bag. He was a short man, but quite muscular.

She yawned and lay down across the seat.

The man continued to fiddle with the catch on his zipper.

She closed her eyes.

He slowly kicked her bag away from the floor.

Katy thought of the beaches and of walking her new black cocker spaniel.

As she lay there dreaming, she felt something touch her face.

She kept quite still and didn't move. She wondered what it could be.

It was large and warm. It reminded her of grandad.

For a few minutes something pressed up to her lip. Then it stopped. She turned her head towards the window. It might have been a hand?

When she opened her eyes, the man was just sitting down on the seat opposite.

Her eyes glanced down to his pants where a pronounced bump protruded forward, hidden inside his shorts, predominantly male.

"You dirty bastard!" she said. "I'm going to report you."

 FIFTY YEARS A HERO!

241

LATE ADDITIONS

What's wrong with shouting anyway

By SARIN | *Published: AUGUST 16, 2021* | *Edit*

Your knee hurts.
You can't sleep.
Someone fiddling in the kitchen all night.
Fifty press-ups on the carpet!

Jabberwock is back…

By SARIN | *Published: AUGUST 16, 2021* | *Edit*

As agreed, I rang the Pain-in-the-butt, so she could speak to mum.
"He's not had very much in life. You have to feel sorry for him."
And you've had plenty, from the age of eleven or twelve, if your diary was
correct, though, I sense, you are not getting very much at the moment…
*Mum has deliberately vandalized the mural I put up in her room.
How I didn't get angry, is completely beyond me.

Benita called

By SARIN | *Published: AUGUST 16, 2021* | *Edit*

Had a baby in her pram.
Looked like a little black doll.
She's been moved inside a hostel.
It was nice to see her again though.

Spoke to Nichola

By SARIN | *Published: AUGUST 16, 2021* | *Edit*

For the first time, really.
I didn't realize she was so lovely.

At last Janet has found an excuse not to speak!

By SARIN | *Published: AUGUST 16, 2021* | *Edit*

'What's wrong with having your own personal workhorse?' I asked.

Why shouldn't the Taliban live by their own rules in their own country without interference from the nanny state. Who came up with the idea that women all want to be teachers or to strut around half naked in the street? I saw Raab in the air-port lounge,, and he said he always found it difficult to pull-out when he was still nice and hard.

The Old Man of Lochnagar

'That was lived through, so this could be'

Printed in Great Britain
by Amazon

65725388R00144